Email, Internet, Web:
The Personal Trainer

William R. Stanek

PUBLISHED BY

Stanek & Associates
PO Box 362
East Olympia, WA 98540-0362

Cover Design: Creative Designs Ltd.
Editorial Development: Andover Publishing Solutions
Technical Review: L & L Technical Content Services

You can provide feedback related to this book by emailing the author at williamstanek@aol.com. Please use the name of the book as the subject line.

Contents at a Glance

Table of Contents

Introduction

Making sense of everything the Internet has to offer is no picnic
for a beginner. The simple truth is that when many beginners are
faced with email, browsers, social media and all that other stuff
you need to effectively use the Internet, they start to have second
thoughts about making the plunge into cyberspace. Perhaps they
think, they are not smart enough or they don't have what it takes
to get on-line and use the Internet but nothing could be further
from the truth. Every year millions of newcomers learn how to
use the Internet and they do it using a guide like this one.

What's This Book About?

To learn how to use the Internet, you need practical hands-on
advice from an expert who understands what it is like to just start
out. By working step by step through each of the technologies
that tie the Internet together, you can learn how to use the
Internet effectively, how to send email, how to participate in
discussion groups, how to browse the Web and a whole lot more.

With this book, you don't have to worry about tons of
background material or filler, I present only what you need to
know to effectively use whatever I am discussing. Instead of
having to wade through page after page of stuff you may never
even use, you will spend your time learning about the stuff you
really will do use. But there is a lot of ground to cover and
learning about the Internet isn't easy unless you actively follow
along. Although this will require some effort on your part, the
plan is designed to be implemented in a weekend. Do you
already see the light at the end of the tunnel? You should.

How Is This Book Organized?

Making this book easy to follow and understand was my number one goal! I really want anyone, skill level or work schedule aside, to be able to learn how to use the Internet effectively.

To make the book easy to use, I've divided it into 12 chapters. Anyone who wants to learn how to use the Internet and its tools effectively should read this book. Because the approach used in this book is ideally suited to beginners, you do not have to be a computer expert to understand and use the concepts examined in this book.

What Do I Need to Use This Book?

The most important ingredient for using this book is a willingness to learn. This book doesn't assume anything and starts you out at square one.

What Do I Need to Know?

This book is designed as a guide to what you need to know to get the most out of the Internet. To get practical and useful information into your hands without the clutter of a ton of background material, I had to assume several things. If you are reading this book, I hope that you truly want to learn how to use the Internet effectively and although you want to learn about the tools you will need to master the Internet, you don't really want to know how the Internet got started, why it got started and all that other stuff that's best left to the history books.

Additionally, because you've already taken the first step in wanting to learn the Internet, I believe that I don't have to convince you that the Internet is this neat, cool, hip thing that you can't live without. Further, to get all this information into an easy to read format, I had to assume you want to learn only what you need to know to make the most of your Internet experience. After all, entire books have been written on some of the individual topics you will find in this book. But do you really want to wade through thousands of pages of stuff you may never even use?

I truly hope you find that this book provides everything you need to use the Internet effectively. Keep in mind that throughout this guide, where I have used click, right-click and double-click, you can also use touch equivalents, tap, press and hold, and double tap.

Thank you,

William R. Stanek

(williamstanek@aol.com)

Chapter 1. Introducing the Net and the Web

Every year millions of people get access to the Internet. New users that jump right in with both feet often have problems learning how to use the Internet and its technologies. But learning to use the Internet doesn't have to be a frustrating experience, anyone can learn everything they need to use the Internet effectively by reading this book.

After reading this book, you will know a great deal about the Internet and how to use it. So go ahead, get started. This chapter provides an overview of the Internet, the World Wide Web, and the tools you will use to take advantage these technologies.

Nothing since the television has caused as much controversy as the Internet. Anyone following the news headlines might think the Internet is the devil's own playground but nothing could be farther from the truth. The Internet is the world's largest public discussion forum and the world's biggest resource library. All public discussion forums have their good sides and their bad sides. All libraries have a few controversial books mixed in with thousands of other books that aren't controversial. You need to look beyond the controversial to see the greater good.

The Internet is all about sharing information and bringing the resources of the world into your life. If you want to use the Internet to conduct research, learn new things, get a competitive edge, or keep up with what's happening, so be it. If you want to explore the library shelves that aren't as popular as the others, so be it. However, never forget that you have the power to decide what you read and don't read, and you can change what you are looking at as easily as you change the channel on your television using a remote control.

The Net Vs. The Web

The Internet is an enormous collaborative effort between millions of computers around the world that are all linked together. Some of these computers provide information and resources. Some of these computers provide entry points for you and I.

Using the Internet, you can access information whether it is located in your community or half way around the world. Just as you can pick up the telephone without having to worry about the massive array of wires and equipment that may be between you and the caller, you don't have to worry about the equipment and technologies that make the Internet possible.

When people talk about the Net, they are referring to the big potato: the technologies, the computers, and all the other things that make the Internet what it is. Although each chunk of the big potato is designed for a specific purpose, some chunks play a greater role in helping you find your way around the world's greatest library. Enter the World Wide Web aka the Web. Without the Web, we'd all be stuck with a bunch of moldy old potatoes that weren't of much use to anyone except a few scientists and college professors.

Often when people talk about the Net and the Web, they act as if the Net and the Web are two completely different entities that are slugging it out in cyberspace. In actuality, the Web is a part of the Net and without the Net, there would be no Web. You can think of the Web as the user-friendly face of the Net. Instead of having to type in strange commands that tell your computer what to do, you can point and click your way through the largely pictorial face of the Web using your computer's keyboard or mouse. For now, don't worry about how this can be done, just know that it can be done. We will begin exploring the Net and Web soon, I promise.

Tools You Will Use to Tame the Net

Taming the Net is easy if you have the right tools and know how to use them. Just as a carpenter's apprentice starts out with an ordinary hammer, I recommend that you start with the basic tools as well. After all, power tools are neat, but that nail gun and hydraulic wrench can get you into a lot of trouble if you're not careful.

The tools that will get you the farthest with the least amount of frustration are those that help you send messages around the world and those that help you wander cyberspace with the mainstream. If your time is limited this weekend and you can't squeeze everything I discuss into your schedule, take the time to really learn how these tools work. You won't regret it, I promise.

Sending Messages Around the World

You will use the Internet's electronic mail system to send messages around the world. Again, who cares how the system works, just know that it does work. When you send a letter to your aunt Peggy, you probably don't spend all day worrying how the letter gets to its destination. After all, delivering the letter is the responsibility of the postal system.

While the postal system relies on street addresses and zip codes to deliver the mail, the electronic mail system relies on user names and computer names to deliver email. A user name identifies a person. A computer name identifies a computer at a specific location. When you put the two together, you have a unique identifier (your email address) that can be used to send messages just about anywhere.

Messages you send on the Internet's electronic mail system are called email. So when you hear someone say, "Did you check your email today?" They are asking if you checked for electronic messages today. Smile and say, "Soon."

When you get connected to the Net, the organization providing your service provider will provide you with an email address. Before they can set up the address, they will ask you to select a user name. Your user name can be your real name, a nickname or any name, such as William or TopDog. Because there are probably a lot of Tom, Dick and William's out there, your first choice may already be taken. In this case, you may want to go with a more unique name, like JohnnyWalker24 or TomCollinsInAZ.

Once you've selected a suitable name, the service provider will follow the user name with the name of their computer to come up with your complete email address. The user name and the computer name are always separated with the venerable at symbol (@) that you see just about everywhere these days. When you put this together, you come up with an email address that looks like this: JohnnyWalker24@yahoo.com or TomCollinsInAZ@aol.com.

I know email addresses probably seem about as friendly as the U.S. Postal Service's zip code plus 4, but hey, I stopped trying to figure out Zip+4 years ago. Now I just write down the numbers I'm given without a second thought, which is exactly what you should do with email addresses. My email address is williamstanek@aol.com, meaning my user name is williamstanek and the computer I am using is aol.com. How do you send me an email message? You use my email address.

Email is stored in an electronic mail box that you can access with a special program designed to help you read and send messages. Email programs don't have fancy names like word processor or spell checker, but they are useful just the same. The email program I use most often is called Microsoft Outlook. You will learn how to use Outlook and other popular email programs in Chapter 4 "Email: The Basics."

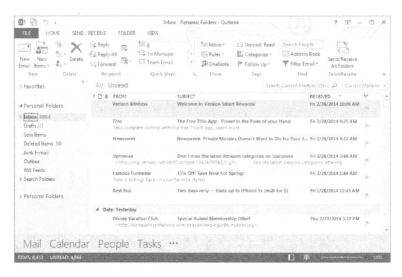

Figure 1-1

Microsoft Outlook: One of the most popular email programs.

Wandering Cyberspace With the Mainstream

Most of your journeys through cyberspace will be done on the World Wide Web. You will use the World Wide Web to wander through the massive library of cyberspace. Scattered throughout the library are files that contain late breaking news, sports scores, stock prices or whatever else you are looking for.

Because the cyberspace library is spread through countless rooms and has books on many shelves, you need a way to find your way around, which is why each file is assigned a specific location in the library called an Universal Resource Locator aka URL. This universal location in a sense points to a specific room and shelf within the library.

Unfortunately, the notation for URLs looks like unreadable line-noise. I mean, what the heck were they thinking when they creating Web addresses that look like this:

- http://www.williamstanek.com/books/index.html

Sort of reminds you of the dewy decimal system your favorite librarian tried to teach you about, doesn't it?

In truth, I know very little about the dewy decimal system, but I still manage to find books. Usually I do this by browsing the shelves. Sometimes I have to look things up in the dreaded catalog, which means I'm faced with Mr. Dewy Decimal. Either way, it is really not that hard to find what you are looking for if you take your time. The same is true for the Web and later I'll teach you how to turn UnReadable Line-noise into something that makes sense.

You browse the Web with a tool aptly named a browser. Browsers display individual pages of information. Like the pages of a book, each webpage can have pictures and text (See Figure 1-2). Although you cannot turn the page of a virtual book, all the pages of the book are connected together and you use these connections to move around the Web. You will learn all the gory details about browsers first thing in Chapter 2 "Surfing the Web."

Figure 1-2

Using a browser, you can easily wander around cyberspace.

Following the connections between pages is certainly the easiest way to wander through cyberspace. However, there are times when you want simply cannot find what you are looking for by wandering aimlessly. Here, you will need to search the library catalogs to find what you are looking for. Because cyberspace is so big, there are many different ways to search and many different types of catalogs.

You will learn how to search for up-to-the-minute sports scores, stock quotes or whatever else you are looking for in Chapter 9 "Working With the Web's Search Engines." Afterward, you will learn other ways to browse and search cyberspace. You will learn:

- How to find the best of the Web
- How to find long lost friends, relatives and others
- How to find businesses in your own backyard and around the world
- How to find fun, cool and free places to visit

Tools You Will Use to Do More on the Net

Sure, you can rely on email and the Web to meet all your on-line needs. You can use email to zip messages back and forth to your boss, your friends, and everyone else you know who is a part of the digital age. You can use the Web and browsers to find programs, read the news, conduct research, and window shop. But there is so much more you can do on the Net if only you take the time to learn how to use more of the Net's tools.

Transferring Files and Accessing Remote Computers

Most of the time you will be able to find and retrieve files using a browser. Here, the browser helps you through the process of finding a file and transferring it to your system. Unfortunately, there are areas of cyberspace that you can't get into with a browser and you will need a different kind of tool to get into and transfer files from these areas. One such tool is a file transfer program like the one shown in Figure 1-3. Definitely take a moment to compare what you see in Figure 1-3 with Figure 1-2. Not as friendly is it?

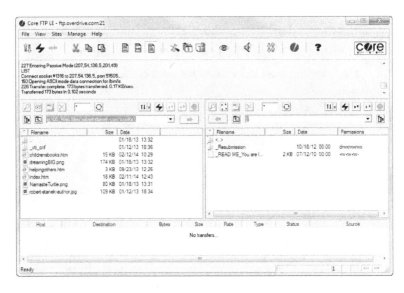

Figure 1-3

You will use a file transfer program to retrieve files that you can't get at with your browser.

When you use file transfer programs, you are moving back in time to a technology that predates the browser. Although the older technology isn't necessarily an inferior technology, most file transfer programs aren't as user-friendly as browsers. The result is that you'll have to work a bit harder to get your files. Don't worry, the payoff is worth the effort and I will do my best to teach you the ins and outs of transfer programs in Chapter 8 "Transferring Files from the Web and Beyond."

Transfer programs are useful, but sometimes you need to work directly with files and directories on a computer that's not where you are. Say you forgot to run a program that prints out the daily reports, only you are already at home when you realize it.

Instead of driving back to work, you may be able to run the program remotely.

Any computer that isn't the one you are using to access the Net is a remote (not at your desk) computer. Accessing remote computers is the job of remote access programs. You will use these programs to perform tasks that you could normally do only if you were sitting at the computer's keyboard, such as printing or creating reports.

Entering Discussions

In the real world, you find people who share similar interests through clubs, associations, and the like. When you join a bridge club, you can be reasonably sure that you'll meet people who are as fond of playing cards as you are. Still, some people aren't at the club meetings to play cards so much as they are to network, gossip, or perhaps even to try to sell you the latest gizmo.

The Net also has its clubs where you can find people who share similar interests. These clubs are discussion forums. There are many thousands of discussion forums that cover just about every subject you can think of. As in the real world, most of the people who join in the discussion are there to enjoy a sense of community and to share common interests.

If you like the idea of socializing on a Friday night and aren't afraid of the Net's wild side, you may want to move beyond structured discussion. In those murky waters on the wild side of the Net, you will find systems for carrying on conversations in real time called Instant Messaging and Chat. Instant Messaging and Chat are a lot like texting on a smart phone. To participate in

Instant Messaging and Chat, you will need an Instant Messaging and Chat program like Yahoo! Messenger, AOL Instant Messenger or Google Talk. Here, each person participating in the Instant Messaging is represented by a picture. Often when someone talks, a comic–strip-style bubble appears and displays their message.

Figure 1-4

Instant Messaging is the Net's version of the office water cooler.

You can think of Instant Messaging and Chat as the Net's version of the office water cooler, yet instead of a chatting with a few co-workers, you can chat with anyone in the world. But be careful, you never know who you are going to meet on Instant Messaging and Chat.

How Did It All Get Started

Interestingly enough, the Internet began as a backyard experiment of sorts. In 1969, the U.S. Department of Defense (DOD) funded a research project to prove that long distance networking could work. At that time, there wasn't a cost effective and efficient way for researchers at various offices to collaborate so someone proposed that the central computers within the offices could be lashed together over a network.

Believe me, a quarter century ago, the notion that you could connect computers separated by hundreds or thousands of miles was viewed as outlandish. Nevertheless, the project got funding and the Advanced Research Project Agency Network was born. Compared to today's Internet, the ARPANET's beginnings were quite humble. At the start a mere four computers were connected together and only one of those computers was actually located a great distance away from its counterparts.

Despite its meager beginnings, the ARPANET was a smashing success—long distance networking really worked and it worked quite reliably. By the time the network was first publicly demonstrated in 1972, ARPANET connected fifty universities and research facilities. The common thread for these organizations was that they all worked on military projects but with dozens of other universities and government agencies eagerly vying for a connection, the U.S. government decided to open the floodgates as it were.

Making room for thousands of new computers meant lots of changes. ARPANET branched out with MILNET (Military Network) and the two networks eventually became the

DARPANET (Defense Advanced Research Project Agency Network). Around this time, a new kid on the block, the NSFNET (National Science Foundation Network), was also getting a lot of attention. The National Science Foundation had set up its network to connect five supercomputers. These supercomputers were the Porches of the networking world and man were they fast, so fast that the existing network connections weren't considered good enough. Because of this, NSF set up its own high-speed network that was separate from the existing networks. NSF made this network available to other organizations in the hopes they would become customers. The possibility of high-speed connections made NSFNET very popular, so much so that by 1990 most of the network traffic was on NSFNET and the U.S. government decided to shut down ARPANET.

Somewhere along the way, the tangled mess of computers and networks became known as the Internet. But what most people don't know is that the name stems from an internetworking protocol developed for DARPANET. Before the ARPANET could be split into two networks, researchers needed a way to communicate between the networks. What they developed was a protocol that made it possible to route information from a computer on one network to a computer on another network—a small feat today but revolutionary back in 1982. Because Internetworking Protocol just didn't sound right, the routing scheme was called Internet Protocol (IP). Today, IP continues to be the cornerstone of the Internet and is used to help route information to computers all over the world.

Chapter 2. Surfing the Web

The Web is the friendly face of the Internet. To explore it, you need only fire up your browser and venture onto the Web. Surfing the Web can be a lot of fun but it is not easy to figure out what to do without help, so take a look at what you need to know to find your way around the Web.

The Browser: Your Window to the Web

You will use a browser to view the Web. Browsers display individual pages of information. Because each page is *linked* or connected to other pages, you can use these connections to move around the Web.

Three of the leading browser developers are Google, Mozilla and Microsoft. Google produces a browser called Chrome. Mozilla produces a browser called Firefox. Microsoft produces a browser called Internet Explorer. These browsers support many different operating systems and have terrific features. These browsers are so popular that over 90 percent of Internet users rely on them every day.

Most PCs, smart phones and tablets have one of these browsers preinstalled. The sections that follow introduce each browser in turn. If you're in a hurry, read only the section pertaining to the browser you plan to use. Otherwise, you may want to read all three sections to get an idea of the look and feel of these browsers. Afterward, you'll head out on the Web and see how you can find your way around cyberspace.

Introducing the Google Chrome Browser

When you start Chrome, you will see a window similar to the one shown in Figure 2-1. Yours may look a little different, depending on the version of Chrome you're using. The browser window has an address bar and a large viewing area.

Figure 2-1

The Chrome window has an address bar and a viewing area.

Focus first on the area at the top of the window: the address bar. Figure 2-2 shows a close up of this area.

Figure 2-2

Taking a closer look at the address bar in Google Chrome.

The address bar can have multiple tabs, with each tab displaying a webpage. When a tab is selected, the first element at the top of the address bar shows the title of the page. Generally, each page you view in a browser has a title, which is shown at the top of the tab. Here, the page title is "Chrome Browser."

Below the page title, you see the navigation options, including Back, Forward and Reload options that I will discuss later. Often items in the browser interface are referred to as *buttons.* So if I tell you to click such and such a button, you will know that I mean to move the mouse pointer over the item and click your left mouse button. Alternatively, if you are using a touch interface, you tap the item.

The next element is the *Location toolbar.* The most important aspect of the Location toolbar is the *Location* box. This box shows the address of the page you are currently accessing in the browser. If you enter an address in this field and press Enter, your browser will access the specified address. Thus one way to get around the Web is to enter a URL—a Web address—in the Location box.

The final element in this area is the Options button, which provides options for customizing and controlling Google Chrome.

Webpages are displayed in the *viewing area.* Anytime a page has more information than you can see right now, there will be *scrollbars* that let you access other areas of the page. To use a scrollbar, click on it and hold the mouse button, and then drag the pointer in the direction you want to move.

At the bottom of the browser window is a *status bar*. The status bar—as the name implies—tells you what the browser is doing. If the browser is accessing a page, you will see a message that tells you the browser is contacting such and such a computer. After contacting the computer, the browser will wait for a reply. When the browser gets a reply, the browser will start to retrieve the page, its images, and other elements. Finally, if all goes well, the browser will tell you it is finished loading the page.

Introducing the Mozilla Firefox Browser

When you start Firefox, you will see a window similar to the one shown in Figure 2-3. Again, yours may look a little different, depending on the version of Firefox you're using. The browser window has an address bar and a large viewing area.

Figure 2-3

The Firefox window has an address bar and a viewing area.

Focus first on the area at the top of the window: the address bar. Figure 2-4 shows a close up of this area.

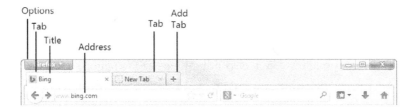

Figure 2-4

Taking a closer look at the address bar in Mozilla Firefox.

As with Google Chrome, the address bar can have multiple tabs, with each tab displaying a webpage. When a tab is selected, the first element at the top of the address bar shows the title of the page. Generally, each page you view in a browser has a title, which is shown at the top of the tab. Here, the page title is "Bing." Bing is one of many search engines available on the Web. You can use Bing and other search engines to find websites and information.

Below the page title, you'll find Back and Forward buttons, which I discuss later. The next element is the *Location toolbar*. The most important aspect of the Location toolbar is the *Location* box. This box shows the address of the page you are currently accessing in the browser. If you enter an address in this field and press Enter, your browser will access the specified address.

Like Google Chrome, Mozilla Firefox also has an Options button, which provides options for customizing and controlling the browser.

Webpages are displayed in the *viewing area.* Anytime a page has more information than you can see right now, there will be *scrollbars* that let you access other areas of the page. To use a scrollbar, click on it and hold the mouse button, and then drag the pointer in the direction you want to move.

At the bottom of the browser window is a *status bar.* The status bar—as the name implies—tells you what the browser is doing. If the browser is accessing a page, you will see a message that tells you the browser is contacting such and such a computer. After contacting the computer, the browser will wait for a reply. When the browser gets a reply, the browser will start to retrieve the page, its images, and other elements. Finally, if all goes well, the browser will tell you it is finished loading the page.

Introducing the Internet Explorer Browser

The Internet Explorer window is similar to both Chrome and Firefox, with some important but subtle differences. When you start Internet Explorer, you will see a window similar to the one shown in Figure 2-5. Again, the browser window is divided into an address area and a large viewing area.

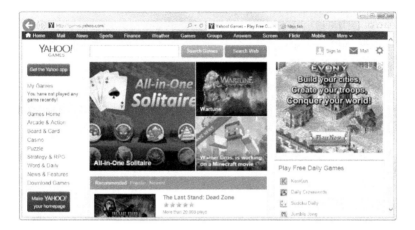

Figure 2-5

The Internet Explorer window has an address bar and a viewing area.

Look at the area at the top of the window first: the address bar. Figure 2-6 shows a breakdown of the elements in this area.

Figure 2-6

Taking a closer look at the address bar in Internet Explorer.

As with Google Chrome and Mozilla Firefox, the address bar can have multiple tabs, with each tab displaying a webpage. Each tab shows the title of the page currently being accessed. Here, the page title is "Yahoo! Games."

From left to right, the first elements on the address bar are the Back and Forward buttons, which I discuss later. The next element is the *Location toolbar.* The most important aspect of the Location toolbar is the *Location* box. This box shows the address of the page you are currently accessing in the browser. If you enter an address in this field and press Enter, your browser will access the specified address.

Like Google Chrome and Mozilla Firefox, Internet Explorer also has an Options button, which provides options for customizing and controlling the browser.

Webpages are displayed in the *viewing area.* Anytime a page has more information than you can see right now, there will be *scrollbars* that let you access other areas of the page. To use a scrollbar, click on it and hold the mouse button, and then drag the pointer in the direction you want to move.

At the bottom of the browser window is a *status bar.* The status bar—as the name implies—tells you what the browser is doing. If the browser is accessing a page, you will see a message that tells you the browser is contacting such and such a computer. After contacting the computer, the browser will wait for a reply. When the browser gets a reply, the browser will start to retrieve the page, its images, and other elements. Finally, if all goes well, the browser will tell you it is finished loading the page.

Getting Started with Your Browser

Don't be shy, step right up to the greatest show on earth. Now that you've taken a closer look at browsers, I will dig a bit deeper to help you learn how browsers work.

What the Heck Is That?

Earlier, I talked a bit about the Location toolbar that you use to enter Web addresses. For anyone who hasn't browsed the Web before, Web addresses are enough to make you say what the heck is that? The addresses certainly aren't written in English or are they? Well, yes and no. A typical Web address looks like this:

http://games.yahoo.com/index.html

> **Note:** This Web address points to the Yahoo! Games page.

As you know, Web addresses point to a specific resource or page. To find a page in the great expanse of the Web, each page must have a unique designator that tells your browser how to find it. Part of the address tells the browser how to transfer the page. Part of the address tells your browser the name of the computer that stores the webpage. Another part of the address tells the browser where the page is stored on that computer. To understand which part is which, take apart the previous address:

http:// Identifies the transfer protocol, which tells the browser how to transfer the page.

games.yahoo.com Tells the browser the name of the website that stores the page.

/index.html   Names the page to open and tells the browser where the page is located on the website.

Because it doesn't really make sense to have to tell a browser to transfer a webpage using http, most current browsers allow you to omit the transfer part of the Web address. This shortcut allows you to enter *games.yahoo.com/index.html* instead of *http://games.yahoo.com/index.html*.

That said, there are other ways to transfer resources on the Web and you may come across some of these other ways during your exploration of cyberspace. Although I could list all the ways to transfer resources on the Net, it is much easier to remember that if you see anything other than *http://* in a Web address, you will need to type in the complete address without using the shortcut.

More Browser Shortcuts

As you know from the previous discussion, the Web address *http://games.yahoo.com/index.html* tells the browser the transfer protocol to use and the name of the website to access. Although the website name in this example begins with *games*, you'll often see website names that begin with *www*, which is an acronym for World Wide Web. For example, *http://www.yahoo.com/index.html* is the web address of the top-level page for *yahoo.com*.

Just as browsers allow you to omit the *http://* transfer part of the web address, most web sites allow you to omit that *www* part of the web address. Thus, if a website is properly configured, you can enter just the base address of the website, such as *yahoo.com*.

How does all this work? Previously, I said */index.html* names the page to open and tells the browser where the page is located on the website. See the / in the Web address? This slash marks the start of the folder path at the Web site. Just as your computer has folders, so do websites. For example, in the web address http://www.yahoo.com/tech/index.html, the website is *yahoo.com* and the folder path is */tech/*.

Typically, the webpage at the root of a web folder is named *index.htm*, *index.html*, *default.htm*, *default.html* or something similar like *default.aspx*. Again, just as browsers allow you to omit the *http://* transfer part of the web address, most web sites allow you to omit the name of the root page in any web folder. Thus, instead of entering *http://www.yahoo.com/tech/index.html*, you can enter *yahoo.com/tech/*. Great timesaver? You betcha.

Additionally, the root folder of a website, known as /, is always opened by default on any properly configured website. Thus, instead of entering *http://www.yahoo.com/index.html*, you can enter *yahoo.com*. Another great timesaver? Absolutely.

Viewing Your First Webpage

When you start your browser, it will load a default page into the browser window. Because this page is the first thing you see when you access the Web, it is called your *start page*. A start page is like your own personal home page on the Web. No matter where you are on the Web, you can return to this page, simply by pressing the Start or Home button on your browser's address bar.

Usually, you will discover that your start page is set to the main page of the browser developer or the main page of your service provider. Don't worry, you aren't stuck with the start page you see. You will learn how to change the start page setting later today under "Working with Your Browser."

While I'm on the subject of start pages and home pages, you should know that *home page* has many meanings. Basically, a home page is the main page for a person or an organization. Your personal home page is the page you see when you start your browser. Google's home page is the page you see when you access the main page at Google.

You can access a page by typing its Web address into your browser's Location or Address box, and then pressing Enter. This means you can visit the Yahoo! Games home page as follows:

1. Click in the Location or Address field.
2. Type in the Web address. That is, type either games.yahoo.com/ or http://games.yahoo.com/.
3. Press Enter.

Understanding How Pages and Resources Are Connected

Most webpages are connected to other pages. These connections between pages are called *links.* All you need to do is to click on a link to access its related page. Because the Web is much more than mere webpages, sometimes a link you click on will play a song, run a video, or do something else equally wonderful.

The way you tell an actual webpage from all this other stuff is by the Web address. Usually, addresses for webpages end with .htm, .html, or the slash mark (/).

Finding links in pages is meant to be easy, but this isn't always the case. The reason for this is that links can be created with text, images, or a combination of text and images.

Any text in a webpage can be used in a link. Text links are usually but not always underlined or highlighted in a different color from the normal text on the page. To follow a text link, point to the underlined or highlighted text and click on it.

Likewise, any picture in a webpage can be used in a link. To follow an image link, point to the picture and click on it.

You can tell when you are pointing to a text or an image link because the mouse pointer will change to a little hand. Also, the browser's status bar will usually display the address to which the link points or a description of the link. If you aren't sure if something is a link or not, click on it anyway. You can't go wrong; either you will head off to someplace new or you won't.

Figure 2-7 shows an example webpage containing text and image links.

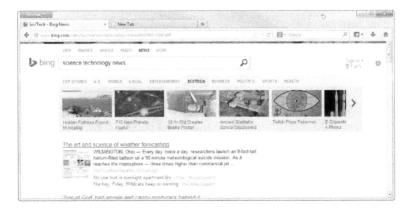

Figure 2-7

Both text and images can be used with links. Here, all the underlined text will take you somewhere, as will the picture of the book.

Some pictures contain more than one link. Pictures with multiple links are called *image maps,* meaning they contain a map of sorts to places on the Web. You will know an image map when you see it because it will usually be quite large and have a lot of text or small graphics built into it. Generally, each section of text or individual picture will have its own link. To use a link, simply click when you see your mouse pointer turn into a little hand.

> **Tip:** Occasionally when you move the pointer around an image map, your browser's status bar will display strange messages that contain a question mark followed by some numbers. These numbers, indicating the position of the pointer over the image map, are used by the computer and you shouldn't worry about them at all. Just know that if you see these strange messages, you are pointing to an image map.

Getting Around on the Web

As you've just learned, getting around on the Web is easy with links and addresses. With links, you simply point to the link and click. With addresses, you type in the address and press Enter. Your browser's menu and tool area provide other ways to move around the Web as well, and there are also some keyboard shortcuts for when you get tired of using the mouse. I'll mention some of them as you go along, and you'll find others for yourself.

Going Back

Browsers remember places you've visited on the Web. Anytime you follow a link you can go back to the previous page by clicking on the Back button. You'll find the Back button on the browser's Address bar. If you forget what the previous page was all about, your browser will usually display its page title when you leave the pointer over the Back button for a few seconds.

> **Note:** From the keyboard, you can go back to the previous page by pressing Alt+left arrow.

In Chrome, Firefox and Internet Explorer, you can get a menu of many of the previous pages you've visited. With the pointer over the Back button, right-click to display the menu. Move the pointer up or down the menu, and then click when your preferred page is highlighted. Keep in mind that these browsers only remember places you've visited since you started the browser. If you shut down your browser and restarted it, the places you visited previously are gone.

Going Forward

Whenever you go back to a previous page, your browser will also let you go forward. To do this, click on the Forward button.

> **Note:** From the keyboard, you can go forward by pressing Alt+right arrow.

Going Home

Dorothy in *The Wizard of Oz* had to tap the heels of her shoes together three times to get home, but all you need to do is click on the Home button once. Clicking on the Home button will take you to your personal home page. I'll tell you how you can customize the Home button later.

Although Google Chrome doesn't have a Home button by default, your home page opens whenever you start Google Chrome. To add a Home button, complete the following steps:

1. In Chrome, select the Options button and then select Settings.

2. On the Settings panel, under Appearance, select Show Home button.

What Happened—Can I Restart This?

Sometimes a page won't load fully or look the way it's supposed to. If this happens, you may want to load the page again. You can reload the page in Chrome and most other browsers by clicking on the Reload button. You can reload the page in Internet Explorer by clicking on the Refresh button.

> **Tip:** Press Shift while clicking on the Reload or Refresh button to make sure you get a new copy of the page from the Web rather than using the one stored in your computer. The stored page may include the problem that is causing it to appear incorrectly on your screen. For more on stored files, see "Managing the Byte-Eating Beast" in the next section, "Working with Your Browser."

Stop—This Is Taking Forever

Another common problem you may encounter when wandering the Web is that a page seems to take forever to load. Sometimes this is because the computer that provided the page is really busy or didn't connect to your browser correctly. Other times this is because there is too much stuff on the webpage. Either way, clicking on the Stop button will stop the loading of the page.

When you think the computer is busy or you don't have a good connection, you may want to try to load the page again. Otherwise, you may want to go back to the previous page or head off in a different direction.

Printing Webpages

Telling a browser to print a webpage is easy, perfecting the process isn't. Start by accessing the webpage in your browser, then tell the browser to print the page. To print a webpage in Internet Explorer, Firefox or Chrome, press Ctrl+P. Next click OK or Print as appropriate to print using the default settings.

As you'll quickly discover, there's definitely a knack to printing webpages. Most browsers tell your printer to print using options that may be less than optimal and may not even be readable. To customize the way a page is printed.

To change print options in Internet Explorer or Firefox, complete the following steps:

1. Bring up the printer dialog by clicking the browser's Options button, selecting Print and then selecting Print Preview.
2. Select Portrait orientation if you want printed pages to be taller than they are wide. Or select Landscape orientation if you want printed pages to be wider than they are tall.
3. Select Shrink To Fit as the print size or scale to ensure that all the text and images from the original page are reduced in size as necessary so that they fit on the printed page. Alternatively, select a specific scale, such as 80%, to

reduce the size of text and images according to the scale you've selected.

4. Select Print.

With Chrome you can change print options by following these steps:

1. Click the browser's Options button and then select Print.
2. Select Portrait orientation if you want printed pages to be taller than they are wide. Or select Landscape orientation if you want printed pages to be wider than they are tall.
3. Although the print panel doesn't have print size or scale options, you can use Minimum as the Margins option to try to ensure that all the text and images from the original page are reduced in size as necessary so that they fit on the printed page.
4. Select Print

Note: Unfortunately, browsers may not remember your printer settings after you quit the program. Because of this, you may need to tell the browser to use specific settings each time you restart the browser and want to print.

Uh-Oh—What's Wrong?

With so many computers connected to the Net and so many resources, there are bound to be problems. The most common problem you will face is an outdated link to a page. Links get outdated when someone either moves or deletes the associated page. Another problem you will probably see sooner rather than later occurs when the computer you are trying to reach is unavailable. In this case, the computer may be down for maintenance or it may have stopped working temporarily.

To help you successfully navigate through these and other problems you will face on the Web, use the symptoms and solutions that follow:

All I see are DNS errors   DNS stands for Domain Name Service but don't worry what the term *DNS* means, instead focus on the cause of the problem and the solution. If you see DNS errors whenever you are trying to access places on the Web, your device isn't configured correctly. Call the technical support number for your service provider. Tell the support staff you need help with your device's DNS configuration and explain the problem.

Contacting host forever   Your browser's status bar reads "Contacting host" or something similar whenever you connect to a different computer on the Net. If you've been waiting for a while, click on the Stop button and try again by clicking on the Refresh or Reload button. If you try this a few times and still can't get through, the server may be down.

File contains no data   Usually this is the result of a script or form submission that went wrong somehow. You may want to go back to the previous page and try again.

File Not Found   The file you are looking for isn't where you expect it to be. Check the Web address you are using and make sure you typed in the address exactly as it was shown including capitalization and punctuation. If the address is correct, the page you are trying to access has been moved or deleted. Try deleting elements from the end of the URL one at a time—that will get you to pages near the old location of the one you're looking for, and you may find a new link to it there.

Forbidden Page   You have tried to access a page or area within a website that is protected. Generally, to get in this area, you will need an account at the website.

Host unknown   The website or computer you are trying to access doesn't exist. Make sure you've typed in the computer name part of the Web address correctly.

My browser stopped working   You may have been disconnected from the Net. Make sure you have a connection. Also, your browser may have crashed. If you suspect this, restart it.

No DNS entry   Don't worry what the term DNS means— focus on the cause of the problem and the solution. If you see an error that says no DNS entry and it only happens occasionally, the website you are trying to access doesn't exist.

Reading file forever   Your browser's status bar says "Reading file" or something similar whenever it is retrieving a file. You should also see an indicator that tells you how much of the file has been retrieved. If this indicator isn't moving and you think you have a problem, click on the Stop button. You may want to reload the page and if so, click on the Refresh or Reload button.

Service Unavailable   The website or page you are trying to get is temporarily unavailable. Try back in a few minutes.

Server too busy   The website you are trying to access is busy. If you really want to get at the site now, click on the Refresh or Reload button every few seconds until you get in.

Server Error   Server errors occur for many different reasons. Don't worry about the reasons, just back up and try again. If you still can't get to where you want to go, head off somewhere else.

Too many connections, try again later   The website you are trying to access is busy. If you really want to get at the site now, click on the Refresh or Reload button every few seconds until you get in.

Waiting for Reply too long   Your browser's status bar reads "Waiting for reply" or something similar after it makes a connection to a website. If you've been waiting for a while, click on the Stop button and try again by clicking on the Refresh or Reload button.

Chapter 3. Working with Your Browser

Of all the Internet tools you will learn about in this book, the browser is undoubtedly the tool you will use the most. Whenever you want to head out into cyberspace and surf the Web, you will rely on your browser to take you where you want to go. As you've seen, there's not a whole lot to surfing the Web. You just point and click to get around, or type in Web addresses. But there's much more to browsing and browsers than the basics covered in the previous section. To truly understand your browser and master the Web, you need to learn more about exploring the Web and how browsers work. While many of the examples in this section focus on Google Chrome, Mozilla Firefox and Internet Explorer, most other browsers have similar features and you should be able to apply the concepts discussed to any other browser you use.

Exploration Tips

Exploring the Web isn't rocket science. You can point and click your way to just about anywhere. But what happens when you hit a page that has more than pictures, text and links? What do you do when you find a page with fill-out forms, frames or something else you haven't seen before? Instead of staring wide-eyed at the screen and wondering what to do next, take a few minutes to learn about some of the types of pages and page elements you may find on the Web.

Tips for Using Forms

In the real world, forms are a part of our everyday lives and it seems you can't go anywhere these days without having to fill out a form of one kind or another. Most forms have fields that you must fill in, such as name or street address. Forms you will find on the Web are very similar. They have fields that you can fill in—and when you finish, you dash the form off to a virtual receptionist.

Figure 3-1 shows an example form. When you take a look at the form, note all the different types of fields, which can include text boxes, password boxes, radio buttons, check boxes, selection lists, and text input windows.

Figure 3-1

You will use forms like this one to create accounts, submit comments, or provide other types of input.

As you see, Web forms have many different types of fields. A form like this one is displayed when you visit http://mail.yahoo.com and then click Create New Account.

You can navigate form fields by pointing and clicking or using the tab key. At the top of the form are text boxes that you can use to input your name and select an email address. To place your first name in the first text box, click on it, and then type in your first name. Next, press tab to access the text box for your last name. Afterward, press tab to enter the user name you want to use for Yahoo! Mail, such as williamstanek@yahoo.com.

> **Note:** You use a user name to sign in to a web service, such as Yahoo!, and get customized features. When you sign up for Yahoo! Mail, the user name is also your email address for sending and receiving messages.

The Password text box is a special text box. When you type in this text box, the characters are hidden unless you select the Show check box.

Another type of form field you may see is a selection list. In the example, the form allows you to specify your birthday using Month, Day and Year selection lists. To make a selection, click on the selection list, and then move the mouse pointer up or down until the selection you want is highlighted. For example, you could click Month and then select January.

Next, you see a set of radio buttons for specifying your gender. Whenever you see round buttons like this, you are being asked to make a single selection from a group of selections. Here, you are asked to select whether you are male or Female.

Some forms may also have groups of check boxes. When you see square boxes, you can make multiple selections. You will know a check box is selected because of the check mark within the box.

Forms also can have text windows. Whenever you see a large text box, such as Comments box, you know you can enter lots of text.

All forms have a Submit button that allows you to send in your completed form. You may also see a Reset button to clear the form and start again. Although these buttons can have different labels, you will find only one button for sending in the form (and optionally one button for starting over) at the bottom of a Web form. At the bottom of the Yahoo! Mail form, you see a Create Account button that sends in the completed form.

Figure 3-2 shows an example of a completed form. As form fields often are validated as you type, you'll often see error messages similar to the ones shown. Correct any problems shows before you try to submit the form. In the example, I need to specify a different user name and add a number to the password before I can submit the form and create an account.

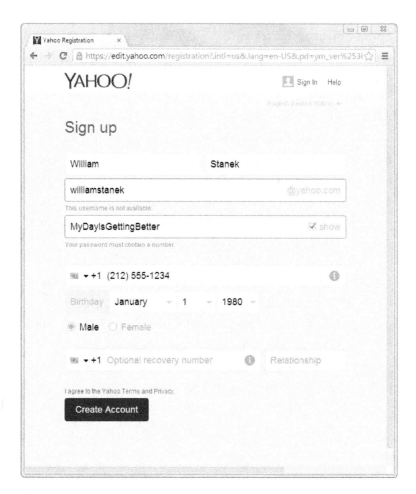

Figure 3-2

You will use forms like this one to create accounts, submit comments, or provide other types of input.

Tips for Using Picture Pages

As you will quickly discover when you wander the Web, there are many ways to put together a webpage. Some pages you find on the Web will have lots of text and no pictures. Some pages will have a mixture of text and pictures. Other pages will have only pictures.

Pages that are completely graphical can be confusing to try to navigate. The first time you visit this type of page, it may seem there are no links and no way to visit other pages. After all, the entire page is made up of pictures—even the parts that you see as text.

To find the links, all you need to do is move the mouse pointer around the page. Remember, when the pointer changes to a hand, you know you are over a link.

Tips for Using Frames

Although webpages rarely use frames on the public Internet, you may encounter frames on corporate intranets. Frame pages aren't easy to navigate without a few tips.

As shown in Figure 3-3, a frame is a mini window within the main browser window that can have text, pictures, and links just like a regular webpage. When you add frames to a webpage, you end up with a page that has several mini windows, and finding your way around these windows isn't easy unless you get a few pointers.

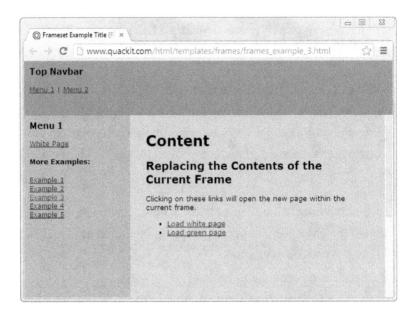

Figure 3-3

Pages with frames have multiple viewing areas.

Anytime the content of a frame doesn't fit in the area designated for its window, the frame will have a *scrollbar.* As if having to deal with additional windows and scrollbars weren't bad enough, links within frames don't behave as you might expect. When you click on a link, the associated page may load into the current frame or it may load into a different frame.

Because links can be targeted at specific frames, you never know what is going to happen when you click on a link. The idea is that instead of having to go back and forth between several different pages, you can use a frames page to help you navigate through other pages.

Tips for Using Layers

With layering, each page can have several layers of information. Usually, each layer of information is placed on top of the previous information to give an overlay effect. In Figure 3-4, the page has three layers which overlap each other.

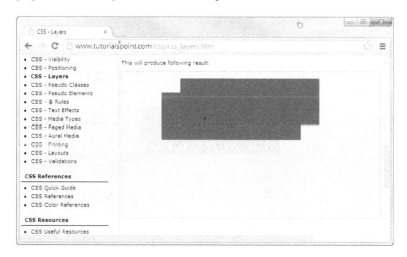

Figure 3-4

Layers are placed on top of each other.

A page's topmost layer, may have a *view tab* or a tab-like extension on the left or right side of the layer box. If you click on this view tab, the layer will be folded away so that only the view tab is showing. To bring the layer back, click on the tab again.

Some large layers are designed like index cards. On the left side and top edge of these layers you find push buttons. Clicking on a push button folds the layer away. To bring a layer to the front so you can read it, click anywhere on the layer.

Anytime you see a plus sign on a menu, you know there are additional options that aren't visible. To see these options, click on the plus sign. After you expand a section of the menu, you can shrink it by clicking on a minus sign. If you click on the left edge of the menu, you can fold away the entire menu.

Tips for Using Tabs

Browsers use tabs to allow you to open multiple webpages. Use the browsers Add Tab button to add a tab and then enter the address of the page to open in the Location box. Although you can use tabs to open multiple webpages, you can only view one page at a time.

To switch between one open page and another, you simply click on the tab you want to view. To change the order of tabs, drag the tab to the desired location by clicking and holding the left mouse button while you move the mouse left or right.

As shown in Figure 3-5, each tab has a Close button. You can close a tab by clicking its Close button.

Figure 3-5

Tabs allow you to open multiple webpages.

Find Lists of Places You've Been Before

When you surf the Web, your browser keeps track of the places you've visited. One way to revisit a page is to click on the browser's Back button, but this only works for pages you've visited since the last time you opened your browser.

What if you want to go to a page that you visited yesterday? Can your browser help you find the page? Yes, your browser can help you and it does this by maintaining a running history of places you've visited before. This running history is referred to as a *history list.*

Chrome's History List

Chrome provides several different ways to access the history list. You can access an abbreviated version of the history list by right-clicking the Back button. When you right-click the Back button, simply select the place you want to visit from the list. To access the full history list, right-click the Back button and then select Show Full History. Alternatively, you can access the full history by pressing Ctrl+H or clicking the browser's Options button and then selecting History.

As you might expect, the abbreviated history list shows only the main places you've visited and the full history list shows all the places you've visited. So if you visited three different pages on the same server, the abbreviated list may show only the main page, while the full list would show all the pages.

Internet Explorer's History List

Similarly, Internet Explorer also provides several different ways to access the history list. The abbreviated list is available on the Location toolbar. You can access an abbreviated version of the history list by right-clicking the Back button. When you right-click the Back button, simply select the place you want to visit from the list.

Alternatively, click on the Show Address Bar button (which depicts a downward-facing triangle), and then select the place you want to visit.

In Internet Explorer, the full history is displayed on the History tab of the Favorites pane as shown in Figure 3-6. To access the full history list, right-click the Back button and then select History. You can also access the full history by pressing Ctrl+Shift+H.

The history list can be organized by date, site and more using the selection list provided. When the history is organized by date, select a date to view a list of sites visited. Each website you've visited is given its own folder. Clicking on a folder will open it and show you the pages you visited at the site. Now when you select an item in the left frame, it will display in the right frame. To close the history list, click on the History button a second time.

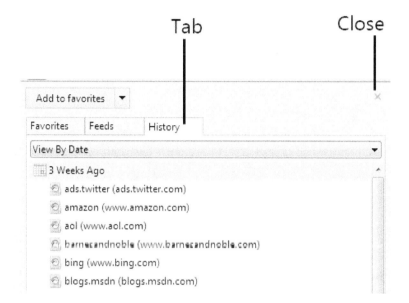

Figure 3-6

In Internet Explorer, your history list is displayed in a side frame. Click on the Close button to hide the frame.

Firefox's History List

Working with history in Firefox is similar to working with history in Internet Explorer. You can access an abbreviated version of the history list by right-clicking the Back button. When you right-click the Back button, simply select the place you want to visit from the list.

Alternatively, click on the Show Address Bar button (which depicts a downward-facing triangle), and then select the place you want to visit.

The full history is displayed on the History pane. To access the full history list, press Ctrl+H. Use the View options to control whether the history list is organized by Date And Site, Date or Site.

When the history is organized by date, select a date to view a list of webpages visited. Each webpage has its own entry. Now when you select an item in the left frame, it will display in the right frame. To close the history list, click on the Close Sidebar button.

Keeping Track of Your Favorite Places

The history list is pretty cool, but it is not easy to track and find your favorite places to visit using the history list. A much better way to keep track of your favorite places is to mark them much as you would the pages of an actual book, meaning you *bookmark* a page when you have it open in your browser. After you bookmark a page, you can revisit it at any time quickly and easily.

Because there is so much to see and do on the Web, most browsers come with fairly advanced mechanisms for creating, organizing, and using bookmarks.

Creating a List of Your Favorite Places

Although creating a bookmark is a fairly easy process, each browser handles it a bit differently. Take a look at how you can create bookmarks in Chrome, Firefox and Internet Explorer.

Creating Bookmarks in Chrome

In Chrome, bookmarks are displayed on the Bookmarks bar, which can be displayed or hidden by pressing Ctrl+Shift+B. Alternatively, click the browser's Options button, point to Bookmarks and then select Show Bookmarks Bar.

The quickest way to create a bookmark in Chrome is to press Ctrl+D while you're on a page you want to return to or by clicking the Star icon in the Location box. You can also:

1. Access the page you want to bookmark in your browser.
2. Click the browser's Options button, click Bookmarks, and then click Bookmark This Page.

Your bookmark will be added to the Bookmarks bar. To delete a bookmark, right-click the bookmark on the Bookmarks bar and then select Delete.

Creating Bookmarks in Firefox

Firefox has a Bookmarks menu and a Bookmarks toolbar. By default, new bookmarks are added to the Bookmarks menu. You can display all bookmarks, whether on the menu or toolbar, by pressing Ctrl+Shift+B. Alternatively, click the browser's Options button, point to Bookmarks and then select Show All Bookmarks.

When you display all bookmarks, a new window opens with All Bookmarks selected in the left pane. Select Bookmarks Toolbar or Bookmarks Menu to display related bookmarks.

To the right of the Location toolbar, there also is a button for working with bookmarks. Click this button and then select View Bookmarks Toolbar to display or hide the Bookmarks toolbar.

The quickest way to create a bookmark in Firefox is to press Ctrl+D while you're on a page you want to return to or by clicking the Star icon in the Location box. You can also:

1. Access the page you want to bookmark in your browser.
2. Click the browser's Options button, click Bookmarks, and then click Bookmark This Page.

To delete a bookmark, right-click the bookmark on the Bookmarks toolbar or in the Bookmarks window and then select Delete.

Creating Favorites in Internet Explorer

Internet Explorer calls bookmarks *favorites.* All favorites are stored in the Favorites pane or on the Favorites bar. By default, new favorites are added to the Favorites pane.

You can display or hide the Favorites bar by pressing Ctrl+Shift+B. You can display or hide the Favorites pane by pressing Ctrl+I. Alternatively, click the Star icon (which is next to the browser's Options button).

To create a favorite, follow these steps:

1. Press Ctrl+D while you're on a page you want to return to. Alternatively, click the Star icon and then select Add To Favorites.

2. In the Add A Favorite dialog box, shown in Figure 3-7, type a name for the favorite or accept the default value (which comes from the page title).

3. On the Create In list, select either Favorites or Favorites Bar, depending on whether you want the favorite to be added to the Favorites pane or the Favorites Bar and then choose Add.

Figure 3-7

You will use the Add A Favorite dialog box to add items to the favorites lists.

To delete a favorite, right-click the favorite on the Favorites bar or on the Favorites pane and then select Delete.

Visiting Your Favorite Places

Visiting one of your favorite places is easy. You can visit a bookmark by clicking it on the Bookmarks bar. If the Bookmarks bar is hidden press Ctrl+Shift+B to display it and then click the bookmark that you want to visit.

With Firefox, you also can open bookmarks by completing these steps:

1. Press Ctrl+Shift+B. Alternatively, click the browser's Options button, point to Bookmarks and then select Show All Bookmarks.
2. Select Bookmarks Toolbar or Bookmarks Menu to display related bookmarks.
3. Select the bookmark to open.

With Internet Explorer, you also can open bookmarks using the Favorites pane. If the Favorites pane is hidden, press Ctrl+I or click the Star icon to display it. Next, click the favorite to open.

Customizing Your Browser

Just about every feature in your browser is customizable. You can fine-tune the start page it uses and lots of other things that will make your Web experience a better one. Not only can you personalize the way the browser looks and behaves, you can also personalize the way webpages look and behave. However, rather than go through customization options you won't use, I will focus on options you will use.

> **Note:** Browser features and options may change over time. However, the general steps you follow to perform various tasks will be substantially similar, even if slightly different.

Customizing the Browser Window

The first step in customizing your browser is to specify how you want text to display. Often, the default font size may be too small or too big. If so, you'll want to change the default font size to help ensure that you can read text.

It's also worth pointing out that every webpage you visit can specify the fonts and font sizes to use for various elements on a webpage. Because of this, you may find that you need to change the size of text on certain sites but not others.

When you change the size of text on webpages, your changes are relative to the font size specified by the site's designers. To make text on the page larger relative to its default size, you use the brower's zoom options. Zooming in or out also enlarges or shrinks the pictures and other graphical elements on the page.

The easiest way to zoom out and make page elements smaller is to press Ctrl and -. On a touch-capable device, pinch to zoom out. When you pinch, you touch the screen with two or more fingers, and then move the fingers toward each other.

The easiest way to zoom in and make page elements larger is to press Ctrl and +. On a touch-capable device, you stretch to zoom in. When you stretch, you touch the screen with two or more fingers, and then move the fingers away from each other.

In Chrome, you can also follow these steps to customize the font size and page zoom:

1. Select the browser's Options button and then choose Settings. On the Settings panel, select Show Advanced Settings. Scroll down.

2. Under Web Content, use the Font Size selection list to specify the relative size of text as Small, Medium or Large.

3. Close the Settings tab by selecting the tab's Close button.

In Internet Explorer, follow these steps to customize the page zoom:

1. Select the browser's Options button and then select Zoom.

2. Choose Zoom In, Zoom Out or a specific zoom level, such as 125%.

Changing the Way the Browser Starts

Odds are very good that your browser is set to start on a home page you didn't choose. Because of this, every time you use your browser, you end up staring at some website you don't want to see. But why should you have to start on the default home page—or any home page for that matter?

Customizing Chrome Startup

Chrome lets you start the browser on a blank page, one or more specified home pages, or the last page or pages you visited. To set the startup, do the following:

1. Select the browser's Options button and then choose Settings.

2. Under On Startup, choose one of the following settings:

- **Open The New Tab Page**   Configures the browser to open a new, empty tab on startup. If Google is your default search engine, the Google search page is displayed. Otherwise, a blank page is displayed.
- **Continue Where I Left Off**   Configures the browser to load the complete set of pages that were open in tabs the last time you used the browser. Thus, if the browser had five webpages open in five tabs, the browser will open those pages again.
- **On A Specific Set Of Pages**   Configures the browser to load the complete set of pages that you've identified as home pages.

To specify a set of home pages to use on startup, follow these steps:

1. Open the webpages you want to use as home pages in separate tabs in the browser.
2. Select the browser's Options button and then choose Settings.
3. Under On Startup, choose On A Specific Set Of Pages and then select Set Pages.
4. In the Startup Pages dialog box, select Use Current Pages and then select OK.

Customizing Firefox Startup

Like Chrome, Firefox lets you start the browser on a blank page, one or more specified home pages, or the last page or pages you visited. To set the startup, do the following:

1. Open the Options dialog box. To do this, select the browser's Options button, point to Options and then select Options.

2. On the General tab, choose one of the following settings for When Firefox Starts:

- **Show A Blank Page** Configures the browser to open a new, empty tab on startup. If Google is your default search engine, the Google search page is displayed. Otherwise, a blank page is displayed.
- **Show My Windows And Tabs From Last Time** Configures the browser to load the complete set of pages that were open in tabs the last time you used the browser.
- **Show My Home Page** Configures the browser to load the complete set of pages that you've identified as home pages.

You can specify a set of home pages to use on startup by completing these steps:

1. Open the webpages that you want to use as home pages in separate tabs in the browser.

2. Open the Options dialog box. To do this, select the browser's Options button, point to Options and then select Options.

3. On the General tab, choose Use Current Pages and then select OK.

Customizing Internet Explorer Startup

Configuring Internet Explorer startup is similar to working with Chrome and Firefox. To configure browser startup, do the following:

1. Select the browser's Options button and then choose Internet Options.

2. On the General tab, do one of the following:

- Choose Start With Tabs From The Last Session to configure the browser to load the complete set of pages that were open in tabs the last time you used the browser.
- Choose Start With Home Page to configure the browser to load the complete set of pages that you've identified as home pages.
- Choose Start With Home Page and then choose Use New Tab to configure the browser to open a new, empty tab on startup. Keep in mind, however, that once you choose Use New Tab, any existing home page settings will be overwritten.

To specify a set of home pages to use on startup, follow these steps:

1. Open the pages in separate tabs in the browser.

2. Select the browser's Options button and then choose Internet Options.

3. On the General tab, select Use Current and then select OK.

Managing the Byte-Eating Beast

Browsers are among the biggest byte hogs you will ever install on your computer. Not only does the browser installation take up megabytes of space on your hard drive, but over time, the browser will use additional space on your hard drive as well. The reason for this is that browsers store the files you access in memory and on your hard disk to speed up the browser. Instead of having to reload the files, the browser gets them out of its *cache,* or storehouse, of files. Although you want the browser to be able to cache files, you also want to be aware of where and how your computer's resources are being used.

Most browsers use two types of cache: disk cache and memory cache. With disk cache, the browser stores files on your computer's disk drive. With memory cache, the browser stores files in your computer's memory. Cached files include webpages, images, and media.

Limiting Space Usage

There are many reasons to limit the space used by the browser's cache. Anyone who doesn't have a lot of hard disk space to spare may want to limit or at least check the amount of disk cache a browser can grab. As the browser cache is a complete record of your web activities, anyone who is concerned with their privacy may also want to limit the browser cache. However, keep in mind that browsers load files from cache to speed things up, so if you reduce the disk cache, you may slow down your browsing experience.

Remember, cache is a funny thing, if your browser isn't set up right you could assign gobs of cache and your browser may never use it at all. The reason for this is that browsers use cached files only when they are allowed to do so. If you or someone else told the browser to never access those cached files, it won't. So before you head off into serious exploration of cyberspace, I recommend optimizing your file usage.

By optimizing the way your browser uses files, you can save yourself a lot of time and have more fun browsing the Web. You should optimize caching based on how you browse the Web and how often page content changes in the sites you like to visit. Only Internet Explorer and Firefox allow you to configure specific cache limits. With both browsers, cache and disk space usage is shown in megabytes (MB), with 1024 kilobytes equal to 1MB.

Configuring Cache for Internet Explorer

When you install Internet Explorer, the browser cache is configured automatically based on the total disk space available. By default, Internet Explorer checks for newer versions of stored pages, images and media every time you visit a website. If the data hasn't changed since your last visit, the cached page is displayed and the page loads more quickly than it would otherwise. If the data has change since your last visit, the browser requests the new data from the website and it may take longer for the page to display.

Internet Explorer also stores a list of webpages you've visited for a present number of days. This data enables autocomplete for the Location box. With autocomplete, locations that are a possible match for what you are typing into the Location box are displayed for quick selection.

You can configure cache by following these steps:

1. Select the browser's Options button and then choose Internet Options.

2. On the General tab, under Browsing History, select Settings.

3. In the Website Data Settings dialog box, the Temporary Internet Files tab is selected by default. Use the Check For Newer Versions Of Stored Pages options to specify when the browser checks for page updates. The default options is automatically, which ensures checks for newer versions of stored pages, images and media every time you visit a website.

4. Before you use the Disk Space To Use combo box to specify the maximum size for the browser cache, note the limits shown and the recommended values for your device. The limits shown are the minimum and maximum values, such as 8MB to 1024MB. The recommended values show the optimal range for your device, such as 50MB to 250MB. Enter 0 if you never want the browser to cache data.

5. In the Website Data Settings dialog box, select the History tab. Use the Days To Keep Pages In History combo box to specify how many days the browser should save the list of websites you've visited. For example, if you want the browser to cache the list of websites you've visited for a maximum of 7 days, enter 7. If you don't want a list of websites you've visited to be cached, enter 0.

6. In the Website Data Settings dialog box, select the Caches And Databases tab. By default, websites are allowed to store caches and databases that contain data that can allow you to use certain web applications when you aren't connected to the Internet. If you don't want this data stored on your computer, clear the Allow Website Caches And Databases check box.

7. Select OK twice.

Configuring Cache for Firefox

By default, Firefox checks for newer versions of stored pages, images and media every time you visit a website. If the data hasn't changed since your last visit, the cached page is displayed and the page loads more quickly than it would otherwise. If the data has change since your last visit, the browser requests the new data from the website and it may take longer for the page to display.

While you can't change these basic settings, you can control the way data is cached. When you install Firefox, the browser is configured to use two types of cached content: cached web content for the webpages you visit and offline caches and databases that contain data that can allow you to use certain web applications when you aren't connected to the Internet.

You can configure cache by following these steps:

1. Open the Options dialog box. To do this, select the browser's Options button, point to Options and then select Options.

2. On the Privacy tab, options on the History panel control whether the browser caches data. By default, the Firefox Will selection list is set to Remember History, which ensures the browser maintains a cache. To change this setting do one of the following:

   ▪ If you don't want the browser to cache data, select Never Remember History and then select OK when informed that you will need to restart the browser for these changes to take effect.

- If you want the browser to cache data but want this cache to be removed when you close the browser, select Use Custom Settings For History and then select the Clear History When Firefox Closes check box.

3. On the Advanced tab, under Cached Web Content, note the value shown in the Limit Cache To combo box. This is the current cache limit. To override this cache limit, select the Override Automatic Cache Management checkbox and then enter the desired maximum size of the browser cache. For example, if you want to limit the browser cache to 50 MB, enter 50. Typically, the optimal size of the browser cache is from 50MB to 250MB.

4. Select OK.

Clearing Out Old Files

Clearing out old files occasionally is healthy for your computer and helps to ensure your privacy. Sometimes your browser will cache a page incorrectly. Other times, you may simply want to do a little spring cleaning and clear out cached files on your disk drive.

Remember, the cache can also contain stored account names, passwords, form data and more. So if you clean out the cache and remove this data, you'll protect your information but will need to re-enter the information the next time you want to log in to a website or are required to provide information in a form.

You can clear out old files in Chrome as follows:

1. Select the browser's Options button and then choose History.

2. On the History panel, select Clear Browsing Data. This displays the Clear Browsing Data dialog box.

3. Use the selection list provided to specify whether you want to remove cached data from the past hour, the past day, the past week, the last 4 weeks, or the beginning of time. If you choose The Past Hour, browser data for the last hour is removed and all earlier browser data is maintained. If you choose The Beginning Of Time, all browser data is removed.

4. Use the check boxes provided to specify the types of browser data to remove. If you select Passwords and Autofill Form Data, you can ensure sensitive account data is removed.

5. Select Clear Browsing Data.

With Internet Explorer, you can clear out old files by completing these steps:

1. Select the browser's Options button and then choose Internet Options.

2. On the General tab, under Browsing History, select Delete.

3. In the Delete Browser History dialog box, use the check boxes provided to specify the types of browser data to remove. If you select Form Data and Passwords, you can ensure sensitive account data is removed.

4. Select Delete.

5. If you want Internet Explorer to remove the previously selected data every time you close the browser, select Delete Browsing History On Exit.

6. Select OK.

You can clear out old files in Firefox by following these steps:

1. Open the Options dialog box. To do this, select the browser's Options button, point to Options and then select Options.

2. Select the Privacy tab. On the History panel, select Clear Your Recent History.

3. Use the selection list provided to specify whether you want to remove cached data from the last hour, the last 2 hours, the last 4 hours, today, or Everything. If you choose Last Hour, browser data for the last hour is removed and all earlier browser data is maintained. If you choose Everything, all browser data is removed.

4. Use the check boxes provided to specify the types of browser data to remove. If you select Active Logins, you can ensure sensitive account data is removed.

5. Select Clear Now.

On the Privacy tab, options on the History panel control whether the browser caches data. By default, the Firefox Will selection list is set to Remember History, which ensures the browser maintains a cache. If you don't want the browser to cache data, select Never Remember History and then select OK when informed that you will need to restart the browser for these changes to take effect.

Tips for Making Your Browser Work Faster

Now that you've cleared out the junk, I am going to waffle on some of the things I told you about cache. Earlier I talked about optimizing file usage and lowering cache usage. Unfortunately, file caching is the secret to a browser's speed, so if you reduce cache you may reduce performance as well.

The problem is that there is a trade-off between the size of cache and the overall performance of your browser. You can improve the performance of your browser by increasing the amount of cache your browser uses. However, if you open the floodgates and accept hundreds of megabytes of cache, you may not have room on your disk drive for other important things. That said, as you know from the earlier discussion, your browser can only use cache when it is allowed to. So even if you have an enormous cache, your browser may never use it.

I recommend using a disk cache size you are comfortable with and have adequate space on your disk drive to accommodate. For example, even though Internet Explorer allows you to set the cache to 1024 MB, you rarely want such a large cache.

If you have a very slow connection, another way to improve performance is to turn off automatic image loading. Although you won't see pictures, you won't have to wait for the pictures to load either, which can speed up the Web dramatically.

You can turn off image loading in Chrome as follows:

1. Select the browser's Options button and then choose Settings.
2. On the Settings panel, select Show Advanced Settings. Scroll down.
3. Under Privacy, select Content Settings. This opens the Content Settings dialog box.
4. Under Images, select Do Now Show Any Images.
5. Select Done. If you want to undo this change later, repeat these steps and select Show All Images.

You can turn off image loading in Internet Explorer as follows:

1. Select the browser's Options button and then choose Internet Options.
2. Click on the Advanced tab. Scroll down.
3. In the Multimedia area, clear the Show Pictures check box.
4. Select OK. If you want to undo this change later, repeat these steps and select Show Picture.

Although you can turn off other features of the browser to speed up performance, I don't recommend doing so. Other multimedia features aren't used that often, and when they are, you usually want to experience them.

Tips for Ensuring Your Anonymity

Anonymity is an important part of surfing the Web. You ought to be able to browse, shop, and play games without having to tell every place you visit who you are. Unfortunately, Web developers found a way to create a trail that follows you around the Web and helps identify you to the places you visit. This trail is created using browser cookies.

What Are Cookies?

A *cookie* is a bit of information that is stored on your disk drive. This bit of information usually identifies you by a customer number and may also track how many times you've visited a particular webpage. Typically, cookies store other types of information as well, such as account information or user preferences. However, for this information to be available, you must supply it. If you don't supply the information, the information can't be stored in a cookie.

Because of the way cookies are created and used, originally only the computer that created a particular cookie was supposed to be able to read that cookie. That meant that website X could read a cookie it created but could not read a cookie website Y created. However, current browsers support cross-site cookies as well as third party cookies. Cross-site cookies are designed so that cookies created on partner sites of a company can be read and used by other partner sites. Third party cookies are cookies created by companies that have a relationship with a website you visit, such as advertisers.

How Do I Get Rid of Cookies?

The big panic over cookies and individual privacy has led people to ask how to get rid of cookies. Well, you can tell your browser never to use cookies or to warn you before accepting a cookie. However, if you never use cookies, you may miss out on some wonderful uses of cookies that will save you time and you won't be able to use the many millions of websites that require cookies.

Some people see the option of having the browser warn them before using cookies as a happy medium between two extremes. You don't have to go without good cookies and can get rid of bad cookies. However, if you decide that you'd like your browser to warn you before accepting cookies, you'll soon find out just how many sites use cookies and how tedious it is to wade through warning messages.

Thus, rather than blocking all cookies or having your browser warn you before using cookies, you may want to configure certain privacy options that limit the ways cookies can be used.

You can limit the way cookies are used in Chrome as follows:

1. Select the browser's Options button and then choose Settings.

2. On the Settings panel, select Show Advanced Settings. Scroll down.

3. Under Privacy, select Content Settings. This opens the Content Settings dialog box.

4. Under Cookies, the default setting is Allow Local Data To Be Set, which allows the browser to store cookies on your device. If you want to ensure cookies are removed automatically when you close the browser, select Keep Local Data Only Until I Quit My Browser.

5. If you don't want the browser to use third-party cookies and site data, select Block Third-Party Cookies And Site Data. Although this option will keep many advertisers from tracking you across sites, it also may prevent you from using automatic logins to websites. For example, you may not be able to use your Yahoo!, Google+ or Facebook login to log in to another web site.

6. Select Done.

Firefox stores cookies only if web history is enabled. You can configure the way cookies are used in Firefox by following these steps:

1. Open the Options dialog box. To do this, select the browser's Options button, point to Options and then select Options.

2. On the Privacy tab, options on the History panel control whether the browser caches data. By default, the Firefox Will selection list is set to Remember History, which ensures the browser maintains a cache. If you want to use custom settings for cookies, select Use Custom Settings For History.

3. If you want the browser to cache data but want this cache to be removed when you close the browser, select Use Custom Settings For History and then select the Clear History When Firefox Closes check box.

4. Under History, the default setting is Accept Cookies From Sites, which allows the browser to store cookies on your device. If you want to ensure cookies are removed automatically when you close the browser, choose I Close Firefox as the Keep Until option.

5. If you don't want the browser to use third-party cookies and site data, select Never as the Accept Third-Party Cookies option. Although this option will keep many advertisers from tracking you across sites, it also may prevent you from using automatic logins to websites. For example, you may not be able to use your Yahoo!, Google+ or Facebook login to log in to another web site.

6. Select OK.

You can configure the way cookies are used in Internet Explorer by following these steps:

1. Select the browser's Options button and then choose Internet Options.

2. On the Privacy tab, use the Internet Zone slider to control the privacy level. When you select a level, details on how the level is used are displayed. Typically, you'll want to use Medium High or Medium as the privacy level.

3. Select OK.

How Do I Check and Remove Cookies?

An alternative to not using cookies at all is to check up on the people checking up on you. By checking the cookies created on your computer, you can see what type of cookies are being created and if you don't like them, you can delete them.

With Internet Explorer and Firefox, cookies are most easily managed through the browser history. Clear the browser history to remove cookies. Chrome, however, stores cookies separately from browser history. To check cookies and remove cookies in Chrome, follow these steps:

1. Select the browser's Options button and then choose Settings.

2. On the Settings panel, select Show Advanced Settings. Scroll down.

3. Under Privacy, select Content Settings. This opens the Content Settings dialog box.

4. Under Cookies, select All Cookies And Site Data. You'll then see a list of all cookies stored on the computer by the browser. Each cookie should be entered on a single line. The first item on this line is the name of the website that created the cookie.

5. To delete a specific cookie, select in and then close the remove button (which shows an X).

6. To delete all cookies, select Remove All.

7. Select Done.

Tips for Making Secure Transactions

Anytime you buy stuff on the Web, you will want to check that the place you are visiting supports secure transactions before you provide any information you don't want distributed elsewhere. A *secure transaction* is a communication between your computer and another computer that is encrypted. When you encrypt the communication, no one can read it without the right decryption key. If you don't encrypt your transaction and you use your VISA card number to order something, someone could intercept the transmission and get your credit card number.

You will know that your transaction is truly secure because:

1. Your browser will indicate that you are on a secure webpage.
2. The merchant has confirmed on the page that the data is sent using a secure transaction.

In Chrome, you know you are on a secure page because the security button on the Address bar shows a locked padlock. If you select the locked padlock, you can get more information.

Don't mistake a secure page for an unsecure one. In Figure 3-8, Chrome is displaying a secure webpage. Note that the web URL begins with HTTPS, which indicates Secure HTTP is being used.

Figure 3-8

Chrome displays a locked padlock on secure webpages. You'll find the padlock on the Address bar.

Internet Explorer and Firefox also show a small locked padlock on the Address bar when you are visiting a secure page. Again, if you select the locked padlock, you can get more information.

> **Note:** Keep in mind that encryption only protects the information. It doesn't prevent the recipient from misusing the information. To be safe, you should be sure that you are visiting a reputable website.

Tips for Doing Lots of Things at the Same Time

Browsing the Web is sometimes a stop-and-go experience that reminds you of driving down a busy street full of traffic lights. The light turns green, you hit the gas. The light turns red, you slam on the brakes. Because many factors affect how quickly you can do something on the Web, you will often find that you want to do several things at once instead of waiting at that red light.

To do lots of things at once, you can open more than one browser window or open multiple tabs in the current browser window. Thus instead of waiting for one page to load, you head off somewhere else and check back later. Or instead of waiting for the sports scores to update every 15 minutes on one page, you open a new window or tab and continue to browse elsewhere.

I discussed tabs earlier under "Tips for Using Tabs." You can open a new browser window in Chrome by selecting the browser's Options button and then selecting New Window. You can open a new window in Firefox by selecting the browser's Options button, pointing to New Tab, and then selecting New Window. For Internet Explorer, you'll need to restart the browser using its shortcut. With all three browsers, you can also open a new browser window by pressing Ctrl+N.

Now you'll have multiple browser windows that you can use at the same time. One of the best uses for extra windows is to browse the Web while you wait for another page to finish loading. Although you can create additional windows, keep in mind that each additional window uses up some of the resources on your device.

Tips for Going Incognito

Although you may want your browser to store history and cookies, you often need a way to temporarily override these features so that you can browse or shop incognito. While pages you view incognito will store browser history, cookies, and search history, this data will be removed automatically after you close the incognito window. It's important to point out though that going incognito won't hide your browsing from the websites you visit, your Internet service provider or your employer.

You can open a new incognito window in Chrome by selecting the browser's Options button and then selecting New Incognito Window. You can open a new window in Firefox by selecting the browser's Options button and then selecting New Private Window. For Internet Explorer, you'll need to right-click the shortcut on the desktop or menu and then select Start InPrivate Browsing.

With all three browsers, you can also open an incognite window by pressing Ctrl+Shift+N.

Chapter 4. Email: The Basics

Browsers are the tool of choice for finding information and resources in the great library of cyberspace, but there's much more to the Internet than the Web. Another big part of the Internet is the email system, which you can think of as an electronic postal system that delivers messages free of charge. That's right, there are no postage fees in cyberspace—none whatsoever—and you can use email to send messages anywhere in the world.

> **Note:** With some Internet plans, service providers may charge you for the amount of data you send using their network. This is especially true with 3G and 4G cellular plans from wireless service providers.

After you use email for a while, you may wonder why in the world you didn't start sooner. Not only is email free—unlike the telephone or standard mail—when you use email, you don't have to worry about disturbing someone during dinner and you don't have to wait on the postman either.

Whoever Said Email Made Sense?

Email wasn't created to make sense. Don't try to puzzle through why email works or how email works, just know that it does work. After all, you don't stop to think about how the postal system works every time you send a letter, yet millions of pieces of mail still manage to get to their destinations every day. Thus, instead of dwelling on how email works, I will show you how you can use email.

You will use email to send and receive messages over the Internet. Unlike regular mail that is directed to a single recipient, email messages can go to multiple recipients. The reason for this is that the electronic postman is smart enough to route your message wherever it needs to go and will make copies of the message for others if necessary. Following this, you could send a single message to everyone in your kayaking group telling them this week's meeting is at 7 P.M. instead of 6 P.M. All you would need to know is the email address of each member in the group.

As you may recall from the discussion in Chapter 1, an email address is created by combining a user name with a computer domain name. The user name and the domain name are always separated by the at symbol (@). My email address is WilliamStanek@aol.com, which means my user name is WilliamStanek and my computer's name is aol.com. You can send me email by using my email address.

Anytime someone sends you email, the message is stored in an email box on your service provider's computer. To read your mail, you will need to access this email box using an email program. The email program retrieves the mail and delivers it to your desktop. When you want to send someone an email message, you will use the email program to help you create and send the message. The email program passes your message off to the service provider's computer, which in turn delivers the message.

Email is kind of cool when you think about it. You can create an email message and send it someone any time of the day or night. The message zips over to the recipient's email box at the speed of light and waits patiently to be read. When the recipient has time, they can log on to the Internet, check their email, and read your message. You don't have to wait on the postman. The recipient doesn't have to wait on the postman. You don't have to dial the person's number and wonder if you are going to bother them or worse, get their answering machine for the eighth time in a row.

Working with Email Programs

Whenever you want to use email, you will rely on an email program to help you get the job done. One of the best email programs around today is Microsoft Outlook, but you don't have to pay for a stand alone email program. Before you can send an email message to anyone, you will need to tell your email program a little bit about yourself and your service provider's computers. The process is a bit complicated, so ask your service provider for their email setup document, which will walk you through the steps of configuring common email programs, such as Outlook.

If you can't get a stand-alone program to work or don't want to use a stand-alone program, you can use any of the free email services on the Web, including:

Google Mail   Sign up for Google Mail by visiting http://mail.google.com.

Yahoo! Mail   Sign up for Yahoo! Mail by visiting http://mail.yahoo.com.

AOL Mail   Sign up for AOL Mail by visiting http://mail.aol.com.

The great thing about these services is that all you need to do to get email to work is to sign up for the service and log in to your account.

Creating Your First Email Message

Whether you are using a stand-alone email program or an email service, the process of creating and sending email messages is the same. Email messages have six basic parts. If you understand these basic parts and how to use them, creating your first email message will be easy.

As a reference point for the discussion, review Figure 4-1, which shows the New Email window of Microsoft Outlook. Select New Email on the Home tab to open this window.

Figure 4-1

Creating a new email message with an email program.

With Yahoo! Mail, Google Mail and AOL Mail, you'll need to sign in to the service to read and send email. Although each service has slightly different options, all three services have a Compose button that you use to start a new email.

Figure 4-2 shows a new message in Yahoo! Mail. With Yahoo! Mail, Google Mail and AOL Mail only the To and Subject fields are displayed by default. If you want to add CC or BCC fields, you'll need to select Show CC or Show BCC buttons.

Figure 4-2

Creating a new email message with an email service.

To Whom It May Concern

The first part of any mail message is the To field. In the To field, you enter the email address of the recipient, such as john_doe@nowhere.com. Pretty easy, I know, but there's a bit more.

Often you may want to send the same email message to more than one person. Email programs are set up to handle this scenario quite well, and all you need to do is to place a comma between each pair of addresses, such as:

- john_doe@imaginedlands.com
- topdog@reagentpress.com

Email addresses don't look very friendly. Surely there's got to be a way to personalize your message a bit. After all, if you wanted to address a letter to someone, you would use their name as well as the street address, so why can't you use someone's name and email address in your message? Well, you can.

Basically, you have to tell the email program or service to ignore part of the information you enter into the To field. You do this by placing the person's real name in double quotation marks and by marking the person's email address with the less than (<) and greater than (>) symbols, such as:

"William R. Stanek" <WilliamStanek@aol.com>

Here, the real name of the intended recipient is William R. Stanek, and the email address of the intended recipient is WilliamStanek@aol.com. Later, you'll learn about address books and contact lists to store email addresses so you don't have to type them in each time.

Sending Courtesy Copies

Just as you send courtesy copies of memos to folks in the office, you may sometimes want to send a courtesy copy of an email message to someone. If so, all you need to do is enter the person's email address into the CC field of the message. All the rules for entering multiple addresses and personalizing addresses apply to the CC field as well.

Hiding Courtesy Copies From Prying Eyes

Sometimes you may want to hide courtesy copies from prying eyes. To do this, you will use the BCC field, which stands for blind courtesy copy. Here, blind courtesy copy means that no one but you will know who is receiving the courtesy copies. Kind of cool, huh?

Although your email service may have a BCC text box, the BCC text box may be hidden. For example, in Outlook, you can click the CC button to display the Contacts dialog box, which has a BCC text box.

From Yours Truly

Normally, email programs and services automatically enter your personal information in the From field of the email message. Although you don't see it in the original message as you create it, this field is there nonetheless. The value for the From field is obtained by combining your name and email address to come up with a From field that looks like this:

"William R. Stanek" <William@aol.com>

Choosing a Subject

The subject line is an important part of any email message. Email programs summarize messages according to subject. Most people reading email messages look to the subject line before they read the message. If the message is from someone they don't know and the subject line doesn't catch their eye, they may discard the message.

Entering Your Message

After you choose a subject, you can enter your message. Your message can be anything you want it to be, but don't send anything over the Net that you wouldn't write down on paper. The recipient may hang on to the email message and it may come back to haunt you some day.

Figure 4-2 shows an example of a completed email message. Once you complete your message, select Send to mail the message and send it on its way.

Figure 4-3

Address and complete the message before you send it.

Sending Mail to Anyone and Everyone

Now that you know the basic parts of email messages, it is time to send mail to anyone and everyone. So start your engines and head off to the Net.

It's important to point out that you don't have to complete and send every message you create. If you need to close the email program or browser window, you can save messages you are working on as drafts. You can then open a draft later so that you can complete and send your message.

In Outlook and AOL Mail, you can save a message as a draft by selecting the Save button. Your draft will then be saved to the Drafts folder. With Yahoo! Mail and Google Mail, messages you are composing are saved automatically as drafts and these drafts will be available in the Drafts folder until you send your message.

Checking Your Mail without Waiting for the Mailman

After learning how to send email, you are probably wondering how you can check your email. As you'll soon discover, checking email is easy; what isn't easy is resisting the temptation to watch over your email box like a mother eagle. With email you can check for messages at any time of the day or night—you can even check for messages on Sunday—which makes it deliciously tempting to check your email when you wake up in the middle of the night to go to the bathroom.

Checking email is easy. Email programs, like Outlook, will have a Send/Receive or Get Messages option. In Outlook, you have a Send/Receive All Folders button, which sends outgoing messages and checks the email server for new messages.

After you connect to the Internet, you can check your email box by clicking on the Send/Receive or Get Messages button. The email program will then access the service provider's mail computer and retrieve your email messages.

If you are using an email service, you check your email by logging in to the service.

- With Yahoo! Mail, new mail is displayed whenever you select the Inbox. Whenever you click the Inbox entry in the left pane, the service checks for new mail.
- With Google Mail, new mail is also displayed whenever you select the Inbox. Whenever you click the Refresh button, the service checks for new mail.
- With AOL Mail, new mail is also displayed whenever you select the New Mail option. Whenever you click the Check button, the service checks for new mail.

There's nothing worse than waiting for a message when you know someone is going to send you something soon. Instead of clicking on the Send/Receive button every few minutes, you can tell the email program to automatically check your email box at specific intervals. For example, Outlook typically checks for new mail every 15 minutes by default.

Answering Your Mail

If you thought having your email program check for email automatically was great, you're in for a treat. Email programs have lots of other extras that make using email a joy, especially when it comes to answering your email.

Replying to a Message

Unlike a letter that you have to address no matter what, you usually don't have to enter address information when you reply to an email message. Your program will fill in the return address for you. All you need to do is tell the email program or service how you want to reply to the message.

You can reply to the person who sent the message directly. To do this in Outlook, Yahoo! Mail, Google Mail or AOL Mail, complete these steps:

1. Select the message you want to reply to in the message summary area.
2. Click on the Reply button.
3. Enter your new message, and then click on the Send button.

You can also reply to the sender and all recipients of the message. To do this, follow these steps:

1. Select the message you want to reply to in the message summary area.
2. Click on the Reply button, and then select the Reply All or Reply To Conversation button
3. Enter your new message, and then click on the Send button.

Note: Whenever you use the reply-to-all option, be very certain that you recognize all the recipients listed in the To or CC fields. Sometimes an email address will be for a group of people rather than an individual—if you include one of those, your message may be sent to hundreds or thousands of people instead of the handful of people you intended it to go to.

Forwarding a Message

Instead of retyping important messages to pass on to coworkers or friends, you can send them a copy of the original message. To do this, you will use the message forwarding option of your email program or service. Forwarding email is similar to replying to email except that the new message isn't addressed to anyone, meaning you must type in the email address of the person you are sending the message to.

You can forward by following these steps:

1. Select the message you want to forward in the message summary area.
2. Click on the Forward button. The email program or service updates the subject line of the message to indicate you are forwarding it. but doesn't let you see the text of the original message. Rest assured, the text is attached to the message, you just can't see it.

   Note: In Google Mail, select More and then select Forward.

3. Enter the addresses of those you are sending the message to and add your own personal note if necessary.
4. Click on the Send button.

Mind Your P's and Q's

The simple fact of the matter is that when you venture into the vast world of email you may encounter people who like to spout off about every little thing. These people send out angry email messages—called *flames*—as often as other people check the time when they are impatiently waiting.

Miss Manners would say to behave yourself even when others are misbehaving and you'll enjoy email much more. So when someone sends you an angry message, your best recourse may be to simply ignore the message. If you feel you must respond, don't do so immediately—wait for a few days and then respond calmly and intelligently.

Acting Like a Net Superstar ;-)

Smileys like winky there in the header play an important part in the world of email. They help you convey emotion. You can use smileys occasionally when you send email to friends or colleagues, but rarely (if ever) in formal business messages.

At times, smileys make all the difference in the world when you want to be sure the reader doesn't take something you said the wrong way. The most popular smileys include:

- :-) Smile, be happy. Generally, means that what I said wasn't intended to upset you. In the context of a negative or sarcastic message means that you don't mean it.

- ;-) Wink. Don't be so serious, I'm kidding. Take what I said with a grain of salt.

- :-(Sad, disappointed.

:-| Neither happy nor sad. Not sure how to react, somewhat indifferent.

:-O Surprise. You got me, I wasn't expecting that.

:-P Sticking out your tongue. Making fun of someone, which isn't very nice.

Some Net superstars also like to use abbreviations occasionally in their email messages. Abbreviations are similar to smileys. If you get into Instant Messaging, you'll probably see a lot of these abbreviations:

<g> Grin

<BG> Big grin

AFAIK As far as I know

BTW By the Way

IMHO In my humble opinion

LOL Laughing out loud

OTOH On the other hand

ROTFL Rolling on the floor laughing

No Luck—It Must Be Broke

Encountering errors when you are trying to send or receive email isn't much fun. To help you with email problems you may see, I compiled a list of common problems and possible solutions that you can use whenever you have problems with email:

Bad login The password you entered for email isn't valid. Whenever you change your regular password, you will need to tell your email program about this new password. Enter the correct password.

Invalid password   See Bad login

No DNS Entry   If this error occurs when you are sending email, check the computer name you entered in the Outgoing mail server field. If this error occurs when you are checking your email, check the computer name you entered in the Incoming mail server field.

Return mail: Host Unknown   The email address you used wasn't valid. Check the email address; you may have typed it in wrong.

Return mail: User Unknown   The email address you used wasn't valid. Check the email address; you may have typed it in wrong.

Unable to locate server   See No DNS Entry

Unable to send for X hours   Typically this message tells you that the mail computer wasn't able to send your message yet. Don't worry, the computer will try again.

In addition to errors, you may also face delays. Mail delays are quite common on the Internet and as a result your mail may not get delivered as quickly as you would like. Although you can point fingers at your service provider or someone else's mail server, all you can usually do is wait out the delay.

One thing you may want to consider is to send a copy of your message to another email account used by the recipient. This way, if the recipient doesn't get your message at one address, they may be able to get it at another email address.

Chapter 5. Managing Your Mail

Email is a great way to communicate with friends, family, and colleagues. After performing basic email tasks like sending an email message or checking your mailbox, you are probably ready to see what else you can do with email. Well, there is a lot more you can do with email. If your email box is full of messages, you may want to learn how you can sort your messages or search for a specific message. You will probably also want to know how you can move messages around to get better organized or how to delete junk mail automatically. Not only will skills like these make your expedition into email more enjoyable, they will also make you more productive. After all, who wants to waste time wading through old messages when you could be sending new messages to your pals?

Knowing Your Folders

Whether you work with an email program or an email service, you'll find several different folders designed to help you manage your email. There's a folder called Inbox, another called Sent, and then there's this one called Trash or Deleted Items. By now you may be wondering what these folders are used for and how you can use them, so take a look.

Incoming Mail and the Inbox

The Inbox stores all your incoming messages and thus is the folder you will use most of the time. When you start your email program, you will probably find that this folder is the one accessed automatically.

Junk E-Mail and Spam

The Junk E-mail or Spam folder contains messages that were automatically filtered by the email program or service and identified as possibly malicious or unsolicited. If a message is filtered and you don't recognize the sender, the best thing to do with the message is to delete it. Occasionally, you may find messages that were inappropriately filtered and you can recover these messages by moving them back to your Inbox.

Outgoing Mail and the Outbox

The Outbox stores messages that haven't been sent yet. Anytime you have a group of messages to send or are creating messages when you aren't logged on to the Internet, you can store your messages in the outbox, and then send all your email at one time when you connect to the Internet. Using the outbox in this way will save you time.

Although programs have Outboxes, email services don't. The reason for this is that you are logged into the service that sends your mail, so as soon as you are connected the messages you send are mailed out.

Deleting Mail and Chucking the Trash

Deleting messages is easy; just select the message in the summary area, and then press Delete. Anytime you delete messages in an email program, the messages end up in the Deleted Items or Trash folder. Placing messages in this folder ensures that you can recover messages that you deleted accidentally.

If you access the Deleted Items or Trash folder and delete a message again, the message is permanently removed. If you access Deleted Items or Trash folder, you also can restore deleted messages. To restore a message, do the following:

- In Outlook, you can restore a message by right-clicking it, selecting Move and then selecting Inbox.
- In Yahoo! Mail, you can restore a message by selecting its check box, selecting Move and then selecting Inbox.
- In AOL Mail, you can restore a message by selecting its check box and then selecting Restore.

Filing Your Messages in a Folder

Two important skills to learn are how to create your own folders and how to file messages in those folders. Although you caught a glimpse of moving files around in the previous section, take a closer look at message filing.

Creating Additional Mail Folders

Often you will want to create additional mail folders. You may want a folder for personal messages and another folder for work-related messages.

Generally, new folders are created as subfolders of an existing folder. You could have subfolders under the Inbox folder called Personal Stuff and Work Stuff. In the Personal Stuff folder, you would store messages from friends. In the Work Stuff folder, you would store work-related messages.

In Outlook, you can create a new folder as follows:

1. Right-click Inbox and then select New Folder.

2. Type a name for the folder, and then press Enter.

With Yahoo! Mail, you can create a new folder by completing these steps:

1. Select Folders in the left pane.

2. In the Folders pane, select the New Folder Button.

3. Type a name for the folder, and then select OK.

With AOL Mail, you can create a new folder by following these steps:

1. Point to My Folders and then select Add.

2. Type a name for the folder, and then select the related Add button.

Moving Messages to a Folder

After you create folders, you may want to move mail to those folders. In Outlook, you can move mail to a folder by selecting the message, clicking Move on the toolbar and then selecting the destination folder. If the message is already open, simply select Move on the toolbar and then select the destination folder

With Yahoo! Mail, you can move mail to a folder by following these steps:

1. In the Inbox, select the check box for the message.

2. Select Move and then select the destination folder.

If a message is already open, simply select Move and then select a destination folder.

With AOL Mail, you can move mail to a folder by following these steps:

1. In the New Mail folder, select the check box for the message.
2. Select Action.
3. Under Move To, select the destination folder.

If a message is already open, simply select Action on the toolbar and then under Move To, select a destination folder.

Finding a Specific Message

Nothing is worse than having an email box chock-full of messages and not being able to find the one you need. Sure, you can wade through your email box one message at a time in your frantic quest—but wouldn't it be better to use the built-in features of your email program to find what you are looking for? Certainly. So look at how you can find your messages.

Sorting Your Mail

Post offices sort mail with giant machines that read the addresses and Zip codes and then file the mail away into specific bins. When you sort email, you also file messages into specific bins, yet you don't need a giant machine to help you. Even better, you can sort your messages in many different ways and all at the touch of a button.

To understand how you can sort mail, take another look at the message summary area used by your mail program or service. Both summarize different categories of information for your messages. Initially, Outlook and AOL Mail use three main category headings: From, Subject, and Received. If you are looking for a message with a specific subject, you would click on the Subject category header. The first time you click on the Subject header, your email program will sort the messages by subject in descending order (as indicated by a tiny down arrow). Click on the Subject header again and your email program will sort the messages by subject in ascending order (as indicated by a tiny up arrow).

With Yahoo! Mail, you can sort using View options. When you are working with the Inbox, select View and then select a Sort By option. For example, by default, messages are sorted so the most recent messages are listed first. If you'd rather have the most recent messages listed last, you can change the sorting order for the Date category by selecting Date. If messages are reverse sorted by Date, you can change back to the normal sort order by selecting Date again.

Searching Your Mail

Sorting is a quick and easy way to find messages, but sometimes you need more—and when you do, you can rely on the search features of your email program or service to come to the rescue. Say you remember that the message you are looking for contained the word Michigan, but can't remember anything else concrete about it. Never fear, you can search all your messages for this word. You could also search for a message sent last Tuesday or a message sent by someone whose user name is William but you can't remember the full email address.

Whether you are working with Outlook, Yahoo! Mail, Google Mail or AOL Mail, you search in the same way. You type the keyword or keywords you want to search for in a search box and then press Enter. A keyword is simply the text you want to search for.

Here are some quick tips that will help you search your mailbox:

- Email addresses   Enter only the part of the address you are sure of. If you know the person's user name is William, use this as your search keyword.
- Subject line or message text   Search on a specific and unique keyword. If you remember the subject had something to do with tickets, use the keyword ticket as your search text.
- Date   You use dates to limit the search to a specific time frame. If you think the message was sent last Tuesday, you may do well to search on all dates for that week.

Filing Your Messages Automatically

Just as email programs and services have built-in mechanisms to help you search and sort your mail, they can also help you file your messages away automatically. As you start to use email more and more, you may find that automatic mail filing is invaluable, especially if you use email at work. I can't tell you how many times message filing has helped me stay on track and get projects finished. Instead of getting distracted by personal mail or junk mail, I file this mail away for later, which allows me to concentrate on work-related messages and get back to my other mail when and if I have time later.

What Is a Mail Filter?

Mail filters are the key to automatic message filing. You use a mail filter to tell your email program how to handle certain types of messages. You could use mail filters to:

- File all messages from Uncle Jim in a personal folder.
- Send messages from coworkers to a work-related folder.
- Dump messages from someone who's bothering you into the Trash folder.
- Dump all messages from people you don't know into the Trash folder.

Setting Up Mail Filtering

Setting up a mail filter is a lot like searching through your mail. This is because your email program or service actually searches through each message as it comes in and compares it to your filter options. These options tell your email program what message fields you want to search and what search text to use. When the email program finds a match, it files the message away for you.

- In Outlook, you use rules to create filters. Select Rules on the toolbar and then select Create Rules to get started.
- With Yahoo! Mail, select the More button and then select Filter Emails Like This to get started.
- With AOL Mail, select Action and then select Create A Filter to get started.
- With Google Mail, select the Settings button and then select Settings. Next, choose the Filters tab and then select the Create A New Filter Option.

Sending Files in Your Messages

Now that you are corresponding with Uncle Jim in Tennessee via email, wouldn't it be great if you could send him a picture of your pet or child? Well, as long as the picture is stored in a file on your device, you can send the picture as an email attachment.

An email attachment is simply a file that is added to the end of your email message. Although the email program or service may not display the actual file directly in the message you are creating, they do let you save the file so you can send it. You can use email attachments to send any type of file:

- Pictures, sounds, and videos
- Word-processing documents
- Spreadsheets
- Programs
- webpages

Sending Files in Messenger

Outlook, Yahoo! Mail, Google Mail and AOL Mail make it easy to attach any type of file to an email message. To add an attachment to a message, complete these steps:

1. Select Attach File on the toolbar.
2. Use the Insert File dialog box to select the file to attach and then select Insert.

The email program or service adds a reference to the attachment. Later, if you decide you don't want to send the attachment with the message, you can delete the attachment. In Outlook, you click the attachment and then press the Delete key. Yahoo! Mail,

Google Mail and AOL Mail, you point to the attachment and then select the related delete button.

Saving Files Sent in Messages

Just as you can send files in your messages, someone can send you files as well. Keep in mind that these files can be any type of file, including an executable one. Although most email programs and services will let you run executable files directly, I do not recommend that you do this. Instead, you should save the file to your computer and then check the file for viruses using your favorite virus detection program. Another way to safeguard your computer is to simply not save, view, or run any files sent by persons you do not know.

> A virus is a devious computer program that can cause serious problems on your computer. Viruses can live in executable files (file extension .exe) and files with embedded macros, such as document files for Microsoft Word and Excel (file extension .doc, .docx, .dot, .xls, and .xlsx).

Whenever a message contains a file, your email program or service will display a reference to the file at the end of the message. In Outlook, you can save an attachment by following these steps:

1. Right-click on the reference and then select the Save As option.
3. Save the file to your disk drive using the Save As dialog box.

With Yahoo! Mail, you can save an attachment by following these steps:

1. Open the message with the attachment.
2. Select the Download option associated with the attachment.

With AOL Mail, you can save an attachment by following these steps:

1. Open the message with the attachment.
2. Click the attachment reference.

With Google Mail, you can save an attachment by following these steps:

1. Open the message with the attachment.
2. Point to the attached file and then select Download.

Typically, attachments are downloaded to the Downloads folder of your device.

Adding a Unique Signature to Your Mail

The way you finish an email message tells a lot about you and your personal style, which is why the final part of a message is called your signature. If you're like me, you probably end your email messages the same way every time. Instead of typing your name and title into your messages over and over, you can tell the email program to create a signature for you. From then on, the signature will appear at the end of every message you create.

You can use signatures to add a bit of pizzazz to your email messages. Your signature could contain a quote, a poem, a wonderful insight into life, or anything else you'd like to share with people your correspond with. However, for a professional setting, you will usually want to stick with the basics and a signature of four lines or less. A signature you use at the office may look something like this:

William Stanek

BUGVILLE CRITTERS (www.bugvillecritters.com)

Meet the Critters: Buster, Lass, Dag, Barry, Cat & All Their Friends!

Most email programs and services allow you to create a signature. With Yahoo! Mail, follow these steps to create a signature:

1. Select the Settings button and then select Settings.
2. In the Settings dialog box, choose Writing Email.
3. Choose Show A Rich Text Signature on the Signature list.
4. Create your signature and then select Save.

With AOL Mail, you can create a signature by following these steps:

1. Select Options and then select Mail Settings.
2. In the left pane, choose Compose.
3. Create your signature and then select Save Settings.

With Google Mail, you can create a signature by completing these steps:

1. Select the Settings button and then select Settings.
2. Scroll down. Under Signature, select the second radio button to indicate that you want to append a signature to all outgoing messages.
3. Choose Show A Rich Text Signature on the Signature list.
4. In the text area provided, create your signature.
5. Select Save Changes.

The email program or service will use your signature whenever you create a new message. Because the signature text is added directly to the end of the message when you start to compose it, you can easily delete the signature if it isn't appropriate for the type of message you are sending.

Address Books

If you are like me, you can't get by without your address book. I mean who can really remember the address of everyone they know—and even if you can, sometimes you just can't remember those Zip codes. Because email addresses aren't much better than Zip codes, you probably could use a little help keeping tabs on email addresses. After all, a message that is incorrectly addressed can't be delivered. To do this, you will use an electronic address book.

Using an Address Book

An address book feature is built into most of the leading email programs and services. Most address books let you fill in addresses as you create a message. Generally, you simply select an email address from a list and the program adds the address to the current field.

Once you create an address book, most email programs and services are even smart enough to finish email addresses for you. Smart email programs and services do this by comparing the address text field with the entries in your address book. Say your address book contains an entry that reads: "William Stanek (WilliamStanek@aol.com." As soon as you type in the W, a smart email program would fill in the entire email address. If you don't want to use the address, you simply keep typing.

Creating an Address Book Entry

The easiest way to create an address book entry is to let your email program or service help you. To do this, you let your email program fill in the details for you from messages in your mailbox.

In Outlook, you can create an address book entry based on the email addresses used in a message as follows:

1. Open the message.
2. Select the email address to use and then select Add To Outlook Contacts.
3. Using the dialog box provided, make any changes to the contact as necessary and then select Save.

With Yahoo! Mail and AOL Mail, you can create an address book entry based on the email addresses used in a message by completing these steps:

1. Open the message.

2. Click the email address to use and then select Add Contact.

3. Using the dialog box provided, make any changes to the contact as necessary and then select Save.

With Google Mail, follow these steps to create an address book entry:

1. Open the message.

2. Point to the email address and then select Add To Contacts.

3. Using the New Contact pane to provide details for the contact age dialog box provided, make any changes to the contact as necessary and then select Add.

Chapter 6. Internet Mailing Lists: Kicking It Old School

Mailing lists are another way to share interests and ideas with people who use the Internet. These days mailing lists are often used to mail newsletters and electronic magazines (ezines) to subscribers. If you work in government, education or military, you may have heard people talking about mailing lists. Although mailing lists are an older technology, these large organizations often continue to use this technology. Why? Because it works and it's efficient.

That said, before you kick it old school and follow along with this chapter, you should see if your employer continues to use mailing lists. If so, read this chapter. Otherwise, skip this chapter and come back to it if you ever hear people talking about a mailing list that you might like to join.

What Is a Mailing List?

Mailing lists are founded on the simple notion that there should be an easy way for widely dispersed groups of people to have conversations on the Internet using email. After all, email gives you everything you need to carry on a group conversation, so why can't you just work within that framework. If you want to send a message to a group of people, why can't you just send the message to the group and when someone replies, why can't the message just come straight to you.

Sending messages directly to participants is a brilliant (though not entirely efficient) solution to say the least. Still, carrying on a worldwide conversation and dealing with potentially thousands of email addresses wouldn't be easy, it would be mind boggling. The answer someone dreamed up was a special group address. Using the group address, participants send a message to a single address knowing the message will be automatically distributed to everyone who follows the mailing list.

Some people would argue that mailing lists are inefficient because they flood the electronic byways of the Net unnecessarily. This inefficiency is one of the reasons discussion groups were created. With discussion groups, you sign in to a website that hosts a discussion and all the messages are stored on that server. Discussion groups are easy to use. You simply sign up for the service and participate by posting messages.

Mailing lists are a bit more tricky. They aren't as intuitive or easy to use. I'm not going to argue the points as to which is better, which is more efficient, or even which came first. Both discussion groups and mailing lists are useful.

How Do Mailing Lists Really Work?

As you might expect, some computer somewhere has to handle the task of maintaining a list of everyone who has subscribed and distributing messages to those subscribers. This computer is called the *list server*. The list server usually runs a program that is designed to handle all the mundane tasks involved in maintaining a list.

When you want to subscribe to a mailing list, you will send a special command to the list program. This command tells the program, "Hey I want to subscribe." In response, the program will usually send you a message confirming your subscription. This message may also have a brief description of the list, the do's and don'ts, and the various other commands you can use to get more out of the list.

As wonderful as automated mailing lists are, there are still some lists that are run strictly in manual mode. Anytime a list is run manually, you have to wait for the list owner to submit your requests and messages to the list server. As this can sometimes take a few days, be patient. List owners hate it when you send requests or messages repeatedly. If you abuse them too much, they may remove you from the list entirely.

Finding Mailing Lists

Thousands of mailing lists await your discovery. The only problem is that finding mailing lists isn't easy, especially now that they are primarily used by government, education and military. If your organization has mailing lists, your company website or intranet site should have a directory of the available lists. For example, to find mailing lists for Apple, you can visit http://lists.apple.com/.

To find other mailing lists, you have to rely on a mailing list directory site. One of the largest directories of mailing lists is CataList, which you'll find at http://www.lsoft.com/lists/listref.html. Although directories often change their website structure, the basic functions remain the same in that they allow you to search for mailing lists by keyword or browse by category.

As you'll learn quickly when you wander a mailing list directory, the names of mailing lists don't exactly make sense. So don't try to make sense of the names. Just remember that you'll need to type in the name when you subscribe to the mailing list.

The other thing you'll need to know to join a mailing list is the address of the list. List addresses are rather cryptic as well but they do tell you two things about the list: the list program name and the list server name.

In place of the user name, you will find a name that identifies the mailing list program being used. Because each mailing list program has different commands and features, knowing which program is being used is important. The second element is the list server name. This just tells you the name of the computer that distributes the list. To better understand how these fit together, let's take a look at two mailing lists:

- OPERATINGSTATUS   Provides operating status updates for the US federal government in the Washington, DC area. The address of the list is listserv@listserv.opm.gov. Here, the server program being used is LISTSERV and the name of the list server is listserv.opm.gov.
- HOMEOWNERSHIP-L   Provides home ownership updates from the US FHA. The address of the list is listserv@hudlist.hud.gov. Here, the server program being used is LISTSERV and the name of the list server is hudlist.hud.gov.

The mailing lists mentioned here are meant to serve only as examples. As you set out to work with mailing lists, keep in mind that mailing lists are subject to change and cancellation, especially moderated mailing lists. The problem with moderated lists is that the moderators just get worn out sometimes and no longer have time to run the list. Don't get frustrated, just find yourself a different mailing list. There are plenty of them.

You'll know that a list depends on a real live person when you look at the list's address. Usually, the list address will include some weird flag that directs your commands to the list owner. Although the flags that identify the list owner are as individual as the mailing lists themselves, some of the flags you may see include: -owner, -request, -approval, and -quote.

What Types of Lists Are Out There?

The ability to direct traffic with email opens up many possibilities. You'll find that there are many different types of mailing lists—moderated lists, commercial lists, private lists, read-only lists, summary lists, and more.

These mailing list types are not mutually exclusive. One mailing list may be a commercial read-only summary list. Another may be a moderated commercial list.

Moderated and Edited Lists

There are many moderated mailing lists. With any moderated discussion, a person or group of people is responsible for keeping the discussion focused on the list's topic or subject area. Sometimes the moderator may also edit messages submitted to the list.

Regardless of whether a list is moderated or unmoderated, you really won't know how the list works until you read its messages for a few days. As you watch the list, pay attention to the topics of discussion and how the list is managed. Often, how far off topic the list members can stray is really up to the dynamics of the group.

Some mailing lists routinely stray off topic into uncharted and unrelated waters. Other mailing lists stay strictly and rigidly on target. The best mailing lists are usually those that find a happy middle ground. After all, one of the goals of any discussion is to build relationships with people who share your interests.

Commercial Lists

An increasing trend with mailing lists is commercial sponsorship. The vast majority of commercial mailing lists are moderated and high quality. The idea is that people are willing to put up with a bit of advertising for a list that is well-maintained and actually focuses on the topic at hand.

When you think about it, the increasing trend toward commercial mailing lists make sense. List owners and moderators should be able to reap some rewards for their services.

In actuality, you won't know how pervasive advertising is in a commercial list until you join. As you might expect, some commercial lists read like one big advertisement. Other commercial lists try to keep advertising to a minimum. If the advertising irritates you, all you need to do is unsubscribe.

Private Lists

Another type of mailing list you may encounter is a private mailing list. Although you may be able to obtain the name of a private mailing list, you may not be able to join it. If you find what appears to be a private mailing list, you usually can confirm this by sending an information request message to the list. I'll talk more about requesting information later.

Read-Only Lists

A read-only mailing list is a list you can follow but cannot contribute to. Read-only lists allow the list owner to distribute information to anyone interested in a particular topic. Read-only lists are often used for mailing out newsletters and ezines.

Summary Lists and Digests

A summary mailing list doesn't distribute the individual messages posted to the list. Instead, the list server puts the messages together until they reach a certain size, and then sends out a single summary message.

Another form of a summary list is a digest—as in *Reader's Digest*—where material is condensed or combined. Some lists allow you to set a digest option. When you use this option, you get summary messages instead of individual messages. Subscribing to the digest version of a list is a great way to reduce the clutter in your mailbox. Instead of getting 50 messages a day, you will probably only get one or two messages a day. I'll talk more about how you get a list digest later.

Joining a Mailing List

Joining a mailing list would be much easier if the various list server programs were all on the same sheet of music. Unfortunately, various list server programs accept a slightly different set of commands. Although having to deal with different commands can be confusing, there are some tricks you can use to stay on track and get the most out of mailing lists. I'll point out some of these tricks as I take you through the subscription process.

Getting Information on a Mailing List

Before you join a mailing list, you may want to get additional information on the list topic and the commands used by the list server. You do this by sending an *information request* message to the list server. The response from the server will be a message with a description of the list. This description will either tell you specifically about the list or will include a header file from the list server. Don't try to make sense of the header file.

To send an info message, you address a message to the list server, such as listserv@internic.net. You can leave the subject line blank. Servers care more about commands than they do subject lines. Server commands are usually placed in the body of the message. In the body of your info message, use the command:

```
info listname
```

where *listname* is the actual name of the list. If you wanted to obtain information on the Nerd Alerts list, you would send a

message to listserv@nerdalert.thenerds.net containing the
following command (and nothing else):

```
info THENERDS
```

Just because one mailing list at a particular server sends you a
description or accepts certain commands, however, that doesn't
mean another list at the same server will do the same.

Sending the Subscription Message

Regardless of the list server, the basic subscription process
remains the same. You address a message to the list server
responsible for the list. In the body of the message, you insert a
subscription command. You don't have to tell the list server your
email address. The list server reads the email address specified in
the header section of your message.

> **Note:** Your signature line may confuse some list servers.
> When sending commands, you may want to delete any
> extraneous text from the body of the message.

Mailing list commands vary depending on the server program.
Keep in mind that the name part of the email address usually
identifies the type of list server program being used, such as
LISTSERV.

For LISTSERV, you subscribe to a mailing list with this
command:

subscribe listname yourname

The keyword *listname* is the name of the list and *yourname* is your real name. The whole command would look something like this:

```
subscribe THENERD William R. Stanek
```

> **Note:** You will often see commands typed in all uppercase letters. Generally, command names can be typed in either uppercase or lowercase letters. Further, you may see references to a command called SUB. The SUB command is shorthand for SUBSCRIBE.

For other list server programs, you typically subscribe to a mailing list with this command:

```
subscribe listname
```

Sample command:

```
subscribe THENERDS
```

If you send subscription commands to the list owner rather than the list, you will know that the list is run in manual mode. You'll know the message is directed at the owner because of a flag added to the address. The two most common flags are -owner and -request. So if you had to send a subscribe request to thenerds-request@nerdalert.thenerds.net, you would know that the list isn't automated.

Checking the Confirmation Message

To ensure that you are who you claim to be, many list servers have a two-part subscription process. A two-part subscription process goes like this: You send in a subscription message. The list server sends back a message asking you to confirm your subscription. You confirm the subscription.

Follow the instructions in the confirmation message. Generally, all you have to do is reply to the message and insert the single word OK into the body of the message. All other text should be deleted from the message. Soon after you confirm the subscription, you will usually receive a welcome message.

Checking the Welcome Message

Most list servers send a welcome message once you are officially a member of the list. For a moderated list, it may take a few days to get onto the list and receive a welcome message.

The welcome message contains information about the list and should also supply most of the useful commands for the list. Because list owners control which commands are available and how those commands are used, list commands available may vary greatly.

> **Note:** You may need to refer to the welcome message later. Be sure to put it into a save folder for safekeeping.

Reducing the Flood of Messages

A few lists automatically use a digest mode to reduce the amount of messages the list server has to distribute every day. A few other lists will allow you to use a digest mode if you so choose, which greatly reduces the amount of incoming messages you will see. I highly recommend using digest mode if it is available.

There are two common ways a list server will let you get digests. Both involve sending a command to the list server. As stated earlier, this command should be in the body of the email message. Here is one command you may encounter:

```
set listname digest
```

Here, you would tell the server to set such and such a list to digest mode as in this example:

```
set THENERDS digest
```

Here is another command you may encounter:

```
SET listname TOPICS: -topic+summary.
```

This awful command tells the list server to turn on the summary (digest) mode for a specific topic.

Tips for Sending Messages to a List

You can send messages to any open list you subscribe to. An *open list* is one that allows two-way communication. Note that it is usually a good idea to follow a mailing list for a few days before you post anything. Lurking on a list ensures that you know how the list works, what types of messages are permitted, and the general stuff that'll make you seem like an old pro rather than someone who is just getting started.

When you are ready, you can send a message to a list using the list's address. Usually, the list address combines the list name and the list server name. For example, if THENERDS list were open, you would send an announcement to THENERDS list using the address thenerds@nerdalert.thenerds.net. Here, THENERDS is the list name and nerdalert.thenerds.net is the name of the list server.

Sometimes the list address doesn't follow the standard naming rule. Because of this, you may want to refer to the welcome message for the proper address. In the next section, I'll show you a quick way of addressing a message to a list.

Once you address the message, you will need to enter a subject line and the text of your message. The subject line should point out the topic of the thread you are starting. Although mailing lists do use threads, the notion of threads is not as strictly followed. Often a series of messages will start out on one topic then move to a different topic entirely. All these messages could have the same subject line or more often than not, the messages could have several different subject lines.

Tips for Replying to a List Message

If you don't want to fiddle with welcome messages or typing in email addresses, always keep at least one copy of a list message in your inbox. When you want to send something to the list, select the list message, and then use your email program's reply function. Either the To or CC address field should contain the address of the list. These fields may also contain the address of the message's original author. Check the message you're sending carefully if you take this approach; the rest of the subscribers won't thank you if you send back a copy of a whole digest!

The rules I for replying to mailing lists are simple. General messages should go to the list. Specific questions, comments, or criticisms should go to the message's original author. To ensure that a reply goes where you expect, always check the addresses in the To and CC fields.

> **Note:** Don't reply to a welcome message. Most of the time this message is sent from the list owner's account, meaning your reply may go to the list owner rather than the list.

Get Me Off This List

After a while, you may decide you don't want to follow a list anymore. To stop your subscription, you will need to send a command to the list server. This is one really good reason to keep the welcome message; it will tell you just what you need to do.

With LISTSERV, you tell the server you want to sign off. Send an email message to listserv@*servername*.com using the command:

`signoff listname`

You would sign off the THENERDS list by sending an email message to listserv@nerdalert.thenerds.net. The message would contain the command:

`signoff THENERDS`

Other list server program support a command called unsubscribe. When you send in your email message, don't forget to use the correct server name. Use the command:

```
unsubscribe listname
```

Common Mailing List Problems and How to Avoid Them

Most mailing list problems have to do with improper addresses. Before you send an email message on a roller coaster ride to hundreds or thousands of people, check the address fields. Anytime you see an address with a flag such as -owner or -request, you are directing the message to the list owner rather than the list. Anytime you see someone's actual email address, you are sending a message directly to a specific person.

Your email address may also cause you problems, especially if you change it. Many mailing lists track the addresses of subscribers and only let subscribers submit messages to the list. So if you subscribed as WilliamStanek@aol.com then changed your email address to director@imaginedlands.com, the list server may not accept your messages anymore. If this happens, you will get an error message that tells you only subscribers may post to the list. You'll have to resubscribe to the list using your new email address. As a courtesy, you should try to send a message to the list owner to tell them your old email address is no longer valid.

Because email addresses change so often, you may also see errors concerning messages the list server has tried to deliver to an address that is no longer valid. Ignore these errors—you aren't supposed to see the messages, but sometimes they get routed to the subscribers instead of the list owner.

Chapter 7. Files and Your Web Browser

Whenever you use the Internet, you are working with various types of files—and you may not even realize it. Files are everywhere on the Internet. When you visit a webpage, your browser transfers a file to your computer and displays it. When you send an email message, your email program transfers an electronic message file from your computer to another computer somewhere on the Net.

To help you make sense of all the files you may encounter as you learn how to use the Internet, this chapter focus on files and the tools you will need to work with files. The chapter starts out with a look at the types of files you may encounter on the Web. You'll learn how to make sense of file formats, how to make files usable, and more. Then you will learn about retrieving files with your Web browser and tools you can use to transfer files to and from your computer. Afterward you will learn how to work with remote computers and how to search for interesting places to visit on the Web.

Browsers make file handling look easy. When you want to retrieve a webpage, all you need to do is type in its Web address or click on a hypertext link. You don't have to worry about typing in commands to tell the browser what to do. You don't have to wonder if the browser will understand how to contact the designated Web server and ask for the webpage and all its related files or even if the browser knows how to read and display the webpage. All these features are built into the browser. But what happens if the Web address doesn't point to a standard webpage? What if the address points to a file or the webpage includes a reference to a file type your browser doesn't understand?

Making Sense of Web File Formats and Transfer Protocols

Hundreds of different types of files are used on the Web—and any one of these file types can be referenced in a Web address or hypertext link. Although browsers do a good job of handling various file types, browsers don't handle all file types in the same way. Some file types are displayed directly in the browser window. Other file types are passed off to another application or saved to disk.

Your browser knows how to handle files based on the transfer protocol and the file extension. The transfer protocol specifies the set of rules the browser must use to retrieve a file. The file extension tells the browser the type of data contained in the file.

Help with Transfer Protocols

Up until now, the main protocol I've discussed has been the Hypertext Transfer Protocol (HTTP). HTTP is the transfer protocol used with Web-based resources. Whenever you type in the complete address of a resource you must specify a protocol, such as http://www.tvpress.com/learn_net/.

Other protocols you may encounter include:

- **File Transfer Protocol (FTP)** A widely used protocol for transferring files. Many Net users consider FTP to be faster and more efficient than other transfer protocols. Most browsers can handle FTP directly. A hypertext reference to FTP looks like this: ftp://ftp.pr.com/docs/mf.txt

- **Mailto** Used to start a send mail session in the latest browsers. Click on a link that references this protocol and your browser may create a new email message addressed to the recipient specified in the link. The reference mailto:williamstanek@aol.com, tells your browser to address a new message to WilliamStanek@aol.com. After you enter a subject line and your message text, you can send the message just as you would any other email message.
- **Telnet** An older Internet protocol for accessing remote computers. When you click on a link that references Telnet, your browser will try to start a Telnet session. As with news, your browser will rely on another program to handle the Telnet session. A reference to Telnet looks like this: telnet://pr.com/.
- **File** A protocol used to access files on a local disk drive. The referenced file must be on your file system. If the file is in a format your browser can handle directly, the browser will display the file. A reference to a local file looks like this: file:///C|/hello.htm.

Help with File Formats

On the Net there are many different types of data. You'll find video files, audio files, text files, and lots of other types of files. As if having to deal with many different types of data wasn't bad enough, the same types of data can be stored in different formats. For text alone, there are dozens of different file formats and all these formats can definitely confuse your browser.

It wasn't that long ago that browsers only knew how to use a few different file formats. Fortunately, browsers are improving all the time. Today's browsers understand many different file formats and if they don't understand a file format, most browsers are smart enough to check for another program that may be able to handle the file.

Programs that handle files for a browser are called *helper applications.* Some helper applications plug into the browser and extend the browser's functionality, which allows the file to be handled within the browser. Other helper applications run as external programs, which means the file is handled separately outside the browser. Helper applications are often used to listen to sound files or view movie clips that are available on the Web.

Because some helper applications plug into a browser, they are also called *plug-ins.* Chrome, Firefox and Internet Explorer support plug-ins. Another type of help application is a *control.* A control is so named because it controls what a browser can do. Internet Explorer is the primary browser that uses controls.

Following this discussion, a video file could be handled in one of several different ways. If the browser supports the file format, the browser could display the video directly. If the browser doesn't support the format but a plug-in or control is available, the browser could rely on this helper application to display the video.

When all else fails, most browsers display a dialog box that allows you to save the file to your disk drive. After you save the file to disk, you can select an application to view or play the file. If you come across a file type that your browser doesn't support in any way, but you would like it to, you may want to look for a helper application that supports this file type.

Common file formats supported by current browsers include:

.gif   A GIF image

.hqx   A Macintosh binary archive file

.htm/.html   A webpage in HTML format

.htx/.htt   A dynamically generated webpage

.jav/.java   A Java team program

.jpg/.jpeg   A JPEG image

.png   A PNG image

.shtml   A secure webpage in HTML format

.txt/.text   A standard text file in ASCII text format

.xml/.xhtml   A webpage in XML or X/HTML format

When you access any of these file formats, your browser should be able to handle them directly. Additional file formats that you may encounter on the Web include

.aif/.aiff   An AIFF audio file

.au   An AU audio file

.avi   A video file in Microsoft Video for Windows format

.css   A style sheet describing how elements on a page should look

.dir/.drc/.drx   A Macromedia ShockWave file

.exe   A binary executable file or a self-extracting ZIP file

.gzip   A compressed file in GZIP format

.idc   A database-related file in ASCII text format

.mov   A video in QuickTime format

.mpg/.mpeg   An MPEG video file

.pdf   A file in Adobe Acrobat's portable document format

.rtf   A text file in rich text format

.sit   A compressed file in the Macintosh StuffIt format

.wav   A WAV audio file

.Z   A file extension for UNIX compressed files

.zip   A compressed file in ZIP format

Checking File Formats Used by Your Browser

Most browsers allow you to check what types of data are supported and how the data files are used. Often, the browser will tell you if the data type is supported directly or with a helper application.

For example, the various types of data Internet Explorer supports are summarized with options in the Advanced tab of the Internet Options dialog box. You can examine these data types by selecting the browser's Options button, selecting Internet Options, and then clicking on the Advanced tab. Settings in the Multimedia area of this tab determine how images, audio, video, and animation are handled. Options in the security area determine whether your browser can handle secure HTML files.

Learning about Compressed Files

Files are compressed to save space and reduce the amount of time it takes to transfer files over the Internet. When you compress a file, you squeeze the extra room out of the file and make the resulting compressed file smaller. Often, compression allows you to reduce the file size by 50 percent or more, which means a 1MB (1024KB) file can often be reduced to a .5MB (512KB) or less.

While compression is great, compression alone isn't enough to make transferring files convenient. After all, a single application may have dozens or hundreds of files associated with it and you certainly wouldn't want to have to transfer each of them separately. To make file transfers more convenient, groups of files are often compressed into a single batch file called an *archive.* Archiving got its start with tape storage devices, when you would store groups of data or files on a tape for later retrieval.

The program you will use to compress files is a *compression utility.* A compression utility can take a group of designated files and create a single compressed archive file. Once you create the compressed archive, your files are ready for storage or transfer. Before you can use the compressed files, you will need to decompress the files. For this task, you will need a decompression utility. Most of the time, the compression and decompression utilities are just different versions of the same program.

Previously, I listed some of the common compression formats including ZIP, GZIP, TAR, and SIT. Although all these formats are widely used, the compression format you use or see the most usually depends on the type of computer you use.

What Is Zip?

On Windows-based computers, the most commonly used compression format is ZIP. Although the most common extension for ZIP files is .zip, you may also see self-extracting ZIP files with the .exe extension. As the term implies, a self-extracting ZIP file knows how to extract (decompress) itself.

Most Windows-based ZIP utilities handle compression and decompression in the same program. The ZIP format is so popular that there are ZIP and UNZIP utilities for other types of computers including Macintosh and UNIX. However, just because you can use ZIP on a Mac or UNIX computer doesn't mean that is the best format for you to use. As you'll see, there are other compression formats that are more widely used on these computer systems.

What Are GZIP, and TAR?

UNIX is such a diverse environment that it should come as no surprise to find several different compression formats in widespread use. File compression is considered so valuable in UNIX-land that most UNIX computers even feature built-in compression and decompression utilities.

The standard compression utility is called *compress.* When you UNIX compress a file, you generally end up with a file that has the .Z extension. You can decompress the file using a utility aptly named *uncompress.*

UNIX also features a standard utility for creating archive files called TAR. TAR was originally designed as a tape archival utility. As you might expect, you compress and archive files with tar then unarchive and decompress files with untar. Unlike other compression utilities, there is no standard extension for a TAR file.

While both TAR and UNIX compress have their uses, GZIP is the superior compression format. GZIP will almost always generate a much smaller compressed file. If you see a file with the .gzip extension, you will need the GUNZIP utility.

In an effort to squeeze every possible bit out of a file, you will sometimes find files that have been compressed with several different utilities. You may find that files have been archived with TAR, then GZipped or UNIX compressed, and then GZipped (again). Usually you can use the file extensions to tell you what decompression utilities you should use. For example, if you GUNZIP an archive and find files with the .Z extension, you will have to UNIX uncompress those files.

Although there are TAR and GZIP utilities for Macintosh and Windows computers, I don't recommend using them unless you have to. Try to obtain files in a different format if possible.

What Are HQX and SIT?

On Macintosh computers, a popular compression utility is StuffIt. Files compressed using this format have the .SIT extension. Another popular compression format on the Mac is HQX. HQX is a native Mac format for binary archives. Although you can use stand-alone programs to decompress HQX files, some browsers will also decompress HQX files for you.

Decompressing Files

Now that you have learned all about how compression works and the various compression formats, you should find that decompressing files is fairly easy. When you decompress an archive file, you are extracting files from the archive. This creates new files with names that should match the original files.

Extracting files does not change the archive file. The archive will still contain all its files. Because of this, you may want to delete the archive once you successfully install the archive program or otherwise extract and check all the files.

Self-Extracting Zips

If you are fortunate enough to download a self-extracting ZIP file, you can extract the files from the archive by double-clicking on the file's icon. Open the folder that contains the archive, and then double-click on the filename—it is really that easy. Self-extracting ZIP files end with the .exe extension.

Extracting Macintosh Binary Archives

The Macintosh HQX format is widely used on the Internet. You can extract HQX files on a Windows-based computer as easily as you can extract them on a Mac.

Basically, all you need to do is click on a link that references the archive or type in the address of the archive. Once your browser downloads the file, you will have the opportunity to extract the archive. Keep in mind that just because you can extract the archive doesn't mean you can use a Mac program or read a Mac file on a different type of computer.

On a Mac, you can also easily extract an HQX file.

Decompressing Other Types of Files

Regardless of whether you use a Mac or a Windows-based computer, decompressing a file archive can involve similar steps. Keep in mind you can only work with compressed file formats that your computer understands. If you install a stand-alone compression program, the program should specify the exact file types you can work with in the help documentation. However, the name of the program is usually the tell-all.

Whether you are using the built-in features of the operating system or a stand-alone program, often you can extract compressed files simply by right-clicking the compressed file and selecting one of the extraction options, such as Unzip or Extract All.

When you extract the files, you should consider extracting to a specific folder rather than the current folder, as this will ensure you can quickly determine what files were extracted.

Downloading Programs

If you download a program from the Internet, it'll probably be in a ZIP or self-extracting executable file, and you can install the program by following these steps:

1. Start your computer's file utility, such as Windows Explorer or File Explorer.

2. Extract the program's setup files using one of the following techniques:

   ▪ If the program is distributed in a .zip file, right-click the file and select Extract All. This displays the Extract Compressed (Zipped) Folders dialog box. Click Browse, select a destination folder, and then click OK. Click Extract.

   ▪ If the program is distributed in a self-extracting executable file, double-click the .exe file to extract the setup files. You'll see one of several types of prompts. If you're prompted to run the file, click Run. If you're prompted to extract the program files or select a destination folder, click Browse, select a destination folder, and then click OK. Click Extract or OK as appropriate.

3. In Windows Explorer, browse the setup folders and find the Setup program. Double-click the Setup program to start the installation process.

4. When Setup starts, follow the prompts to install the software. If the installation fails and the software used an installer, follow the prompts to allow the installer to restore your computer to its original state. Otherwise, exit Setup and then try rerunning Setup to either complete the installation or uninstall the program.

Chapter 8. Transferring Files from the Web and Beyond

Often when you ask people why they use the Internet, they'll tell you it is because you can find so many programs for free. While freeware and shareware programs are great, there is so much more. On the Net, you'll find software patches that fix bugs in your favorite applications and software upgrades that allow you to get new and improved versions of applications for free. You'll also find trial versions of software that you can try before you buy. To get at some of these programs, you may need to use the File Transfer Protocol (FTP).

What Is FTP and How Does It Work?

Although programs can be transferred with the standard Web transfer protocol, FTP is the preferred way to transfer programs. FTP is also used to transfer other types of files, such as documentation and file archives stored in compressed files. With FTP the rules change and there are many things you need to know to successfully transfer files to and from your computer.

Why Use FTP?

When it comes to working with large files—and program files in particular—FTP is in many ways faster and more efficient than standard Web transfers with HTTP. FTP achieves this speed and efficiency in several ways.

First of all, FTP is a technology that predates the Web. Before the Web, there was a network of FTP clients and servers spread all over the world. These clients and servers followed a fairly basic set of rules for transferring files without all the overhead associated with Web transfers. This streamlined transfer process is still available.

Additionally, when it comes to transferring large files or groups of files, FTP is more efficient than HTTP. The reason for this is that FTP is designed specifically to help you work with files. You'll find that it is just as easy to retrieve a file as it is to transfer a file to a different computer. FTP also makes it quite easy to send and retrieve groups of files. An FTP server doesn't really care if you want to transfer one file or a hundred files.

FTP Clients

To access files with FTP, you will use an FTP client. Generally, an FTP client is a stand-alone program that you will use to transfer files to and from your computer. An FTP client can also help you:

- Delete files on a remote computer.
- Rename files on a remote computer.
- Make new directories on a remote computer.

Most browsers have a built-in FTP client. Using this built-in client, you can access files on an FTP server without ever having to leave your browser. However, the built-in client is only good for transferring files to or from your computer. If you want to delete files, rename files, or make directories, you will need a separate FTP program.

FTP Servers

FTP servers are very similar to Web servers with some noted exceptions. You can access a file or directory on an FTP server using an electronic address that looks much like a Web address. This address designates the name of the server and the location of the file or directory you are trying to access. Although most Web servers are named *www.something-or-other.com*, most FTP servers are named *ftp.something-or-other.com*, such as *ftp.microsoft.com* or *ftp.apple.com*.

Whenever you work with files on a remote computer, there are security concerns. To prevent unauthorized use, FTP servers follow an account system much like the one you have with your service provider. For this reason, the only way you can access an FTP server is to specify a valid user name and password. The privileges for the server account are set when you log in. Because it wouldn't do much good to have thousands of programs that no one could get to, there are both private and public FTP servers.

Access to a private FTP server is controlled very closely. Generally, you will only be able to access the server with a specific user name and password. Many companies set up private FTP servers so employees can access certain files from home or transfer files to work.

A public FTP server is set up so just about anyone can get files. When you log in to the server, you will either use a temporary account or an account named Anonymous. Just because a server is open, doesn't mean there aren't any controls to protect the server. The actions you can perform on a public server will probably be very limited.

Anonymous FTP and Guest Accounts

Because of the availability of anonymous accounts on most public FTP servers, you'll often hear the term *Anonymous FTP*. When you use Anonymous FTP, you log in as Anonymous and enter your email address as your password. Once you are logged in, you will be able to transfer files to your heart's content.

A guest login on an FTP server is usually a temporary account designated for a special use. Most guest accounts have an easy-to-remember user name, like *guest* or *guest1*, and a simple password, such as *aGuest*. At work, someone may give you a guest account on the company's FTP server so that you can transfer documentation to your computer.

Do You Need a Separate FTP Program?

Not everyone needs a separate FTP program. If you are only interested in getting files such as free or trial software, your browser provides everything you need to do this. On the other hand, being able to perform file-related tasks such as renaming files can come in handy. If you use FTP to transfer files from your home computer to your office computer, you may need to delete an old file and replace it with an updated one. You may also want to create an entirely new directory for your new files.

Anyone planning to publish a home page may need an FTP client as well. You will use the client to transfer files to your

Web server. You can also use the client to rename files, delete old files, and make new directories.

Popular FTP Programs

There are quite a few FTP programs available. The FTP program you use will depend on the features you are looking for and whether you use a Mac, Windows, or UNIX computer.

What Features Should You Look For?

Basically, you will want an FTP program that is user friendly and smart enough to help you when you have problems. Some features that make an FTP program user friendly and smart include support for:

- Drag and drop   Drag a file or folder icon from one window and drop it into another. Instead of clicking on a file or folder name then clicking on a transfer button, you can just drag and drop.
- Resume download   Continue a download if you get disconnected or an error occurs during transfer. Instead of having to start over, you can resume downloading a file where you left off.

An FTP program I use is called Core FTP.

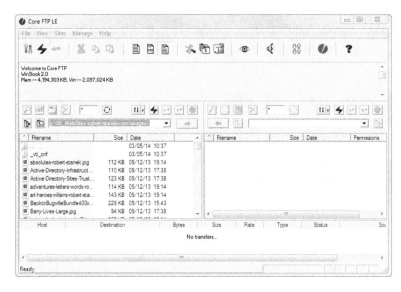

Figure 8-1

Core FTP is an FTP program you can use to transfer files.

Obtaining and Installing an FTP Program

Many FTP programs—as well as many other freeware and shareware programs—are available at http://www.tucows.com/downloads. You will find FTP programs under the heading FTP Client. When you find an FTP program you like, click on the title link provided. Your browser will display a save file dialog box. Choose a folder for the file, and then click on the Save or OK button to begin the download. Remember the name and location of the installation program.

When the download is complete, you will need to run the installation program. Open the folder the file is in and double-click on the file icon to begin the installation process. Follow the prompts. During the installation, you will need to select a location for the software. The default installation options should work just fine, so if you have any doubts use the defaults.

Making a File Transfer

The steps for transferring a file are basically the same whether you use a Mac or a Windows-based computer. To transfer files, you will need to:

- Log in to an FTP server.
- Find the files you want to transfer.
- Choose a transfer method (if necessary).
- Transfer the files.
- Log out of the server.

Logging In

After you start your FTP program, you should see a dialog box that lets you establish a connection to a server (see Figure 8-2). If not, you will need to open this dialog box by using a button or menu option. For example, with Core FTP, you select File and then select Connect, or simply click the Site Manager button on the toolbar.

With the connection dialog box open, you will need to specify the name of the server you want to access, such as ftp.apple.com. Enter this name in the host name or other similar field provided. You may also want to specify an initial directory path on the FTP server, such as /pub/docs. If possible, the FTP program will access the directory you've specified.

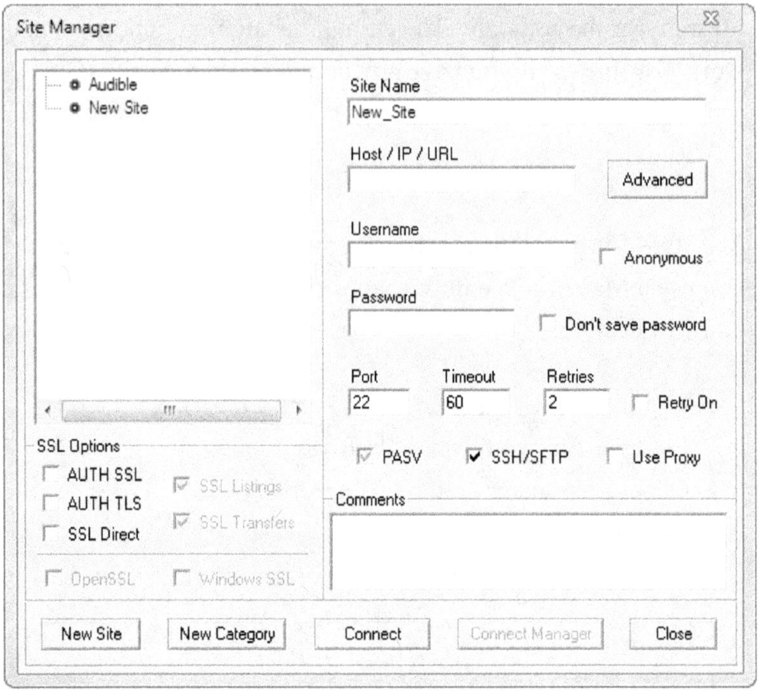

Figure 8-2

Provide the information needed to connect to the FTP server.

Next, you may need to specify the login account you are going to use. If you have an account on the server, enter your user name and password (see Figure 8-3). If you don't have an account, you can usually access a public server with a guest account or Anonymous FTP. Most FTP programs feature some type of automatic support for Anonymous FTP. With Core FTP, select the Anonymous check box. Some other programs are set up to use Anonymous FTP by default so you don't need to enter any user name or password information for Anonymous FTP.

Figure 8-3

Enter the information for the server and log in.

To establish a connection using the current settings, click on the connection option, such as Connect. If a problem occurs during login, your FTP program should display the errors. As necessary, scroll back through the error log to see what happened. Most errors occur because:

- **Invalid login**   You didn't enter a valid user name or password, try again. Letters, numbers, and special characters must be typed exactly.
- **Invalid server name**   Check the FTP server name you used and make sure it is typed correctly.

- **No access to Net**   You may not be dialed into the Internet or you may have been accidentally disconnected. Try to dial back in.
- **No anonymous log in**   Server doesn't permit anonymous log in. If no guest accounts are available, you will need an account for this server.
- **Server is too busy**   If the server is too busy, check back later. Some servers are so busy during the day that it is hard to establish a connection. When this happens, try back after hours or on the weekend.

Finding Files to Transfer

Finding files you want to transfer is a simple matter of wandering around the FTP server until you find something you like. Regardless of the FTP program you use, you'll find that you can browse files and folders on the server in much the same way as you browse your own file system. When you find files you want to transfer, select them just as you would any other file.

Most windows used by FTP programs indicate whether you are on your computer or a remote computer. When the program is talking about your computer, you'll see references to *local host, local files*, or *local folders.* When the program is talking about FTP servers, you'll see references to *remote host, remote files,* or *remote folders.*

Transferring Files

Transferring a file to or from your computer requires similar steps. In both instances, you are transferring a file from one place to another. The main difference is in where the file is going. When you transfer a file to your computer, you are *downloading* the file for storage on your disk drive. When you transfer a file from your computer, you are *uploading* the file to a disk drive on a remote computer.

You download files as follows:

- Find the files you want to download on the remote computer, and then access a folder where you want to save the files on your computer. Ideally, this will be a separate folder that you use for downloads.
- Initiate the transfer. With drag and drop, you simply drag the files from the remote server, and then drop them into a local folder on your computer. Most programs also let you double-click on a filename to begin the transfer.

  FTP servers often have help files. Look for a file named index, readme, or help. Additionally, most of the time program files are saved within a directory called pub. Look for this directory if you can't find the files you are looking for.

You upload files as follows:

- Open the folder containing the files you want to transfer, and then access a folder on the FTP server where you want to save the files. Most public servers have specific rules for file uploading. If you are permitted to upload files, you will usually be able to do so only in an incoming file folder.
- Initiate the transfer. Drag and drop allows you to drag the files from your local folder and drop them into a folder on

the FTP server. You may also be able to begin the transfer by double-clicking on a filename.

Logging Out

When you are finished transferring files you should log out. Use your program's Close connection button or similar feature to say so long to the server. Logging out of an FTP server is especially important because most servers restrict the number of open connections. For example, a public server may allow only 500 connections. If you or someone else tries to establish connection number 501, the server sends a message that says it is busy.

Transferring Files from the Web

Web-based file transfers are the easiest. You don't have to fiddle with stand-alone FTP clients at all. All you need to do is click on a link or type in an address that leads to an FTP server, and then your browser helps you through the rest of the process. Still, different browsers handle FTP transfers in different ways. Both Google Chrome and Internet Explorer have a built-in FTP client. While Google Chrome allows you to upload and download files, Internet Explorer only allows you to download files. This means if you use Internet Explorer and you want to transfer files to an FTP server, you will need a separate FTP client.

How Do You Know a Link Uses FTP?

Addresses for FTP servers begin with the identifier *ftp://*. FTP addresses work much like Web addresses. Click on a link that begins with the *ftp://* identifier and your browser will access the designated FTP server directly. You can also enter an FTP address just as you would a Web address. Type in the URL to a directory or a specific file in a directory, such as:

```
ftp://ftp.symantec.com/public/
```

Just as some browsers allow you to omit the *http://* part of a Web address, some browsers also allow you to omit the *ftp://* part of an FTP address. Instead of typing

```
ftp://ftp.symantec.com/public/
```

You may be able to type

```
ftp.symantec.com/public/
```

What about Accounts and Anonymous Logins?

From earlier discussions, you know that you need to specify an account name and password when you access an FTP server. By default, most browsers log in to a server using Anonymous FTP. As long as you haven't changed the default settings for Anonymous FTP, both Internet Explorer and Google Chrome will automatically log in with Anonymous FTP.

Anytime you need to log in to an FTP server with a named account, you will need to specify the account information in the FTP address. You can specify the user name like this:

```
ftp://fido@ftp.symantec.com/
```

Here, *fido* is the user name for an account on the FTP server at ftp.netscape.com. Because you didn't specify a password, your browser should prompt you for the password.

You could also specify the user name and password for the account like this:

```
ftp://fido:ruffruff@ftp.symantec.com/
```

Here, *fido* is the user name and the password is *ruffruff.*

> **Note:** When you specify the password in the URL, the password may be recorded in a log file on the FTP server. Because anyone with access to the log files may find your password, you should rarely specify a password in the FTP address.

Getting and Saving Files

Regardless of the type of browser you use, you will get and save files following similar steps. You start by running your Web browser and logging onto the Internet as usual. Now you can access an FTP server as follows:

- Click on an FTP address in a webpage.
- Type the URL to an FTP server in your browser's Address or Location field. Press Enter.

Anytime you access a directory rather than a specific file on an FTP server, your browser will show you a listing of the directory (see Figure 8-4). You can use the listing to access other directories and files on the FTP server.

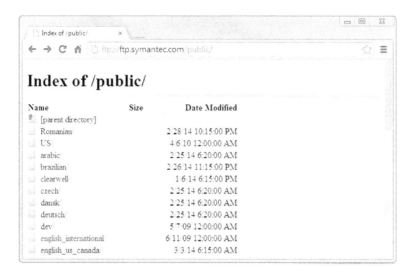

Figure 8 4

Your browser may display a directory listing. You can use this listing to access other directories and files on the FTP server.

Generally, your browser will display files and directories with an icon and a text link (See Figure 8-4). Click on a directory name or folder icon and your browser will access the directory and display its listing. Click on a filename or file icon and your browser will handle it just as it would any other file.

If the browser can handle the file directly, it will display the file in the browser window. Otherwise, the browser will probably display a dialog box that lets you save the file to your disk drive. The save file dialog box should also display anytime you click on a link or type in a URL that identifies a specific file on an FTP server. Save the file to your disk drive.

Uploading Files with Your Browser

Although your browser may you to upload files to an FTP server, you will need special permission to do this. Generally, if you have an account on an FTP server, you should be able to upload files. However, if you are accessing a public server, you can usually upload files only to a specific directory. This directory may be called incoming_files or something similar.

Before you upload files, you should log in to the FTP server and access the directory to which you want to transfer the files. Now just drag a file or a group of files from any other program, such as Windows Explorer or File Explorer, to the browser window. If the browser prompts you to confirm that you really want to upload the dragged files, choose Yes. You should see a dialog box that says the files are being uploaded to the FTP server.

Moving the Furniture Around with FTP

FTP programs allow you to do more than simple file transfers. Usually, you can perform many other tasks including renaming files, deleting files, and creating new directories. While the FTP program is running, you can perform these tasks on your local disk drive and also on the remote FTP server if you have permission.

Deleting Files and Directories from a Server

To delete a file or directory, you will first need to select it. Click on the filename. Next, press Delete on your keyboard or choose an appropriately named button or menu option, such as Delete.

Your FTP program may ask you to confirm that you want to delete the file or directory. Click on Yes or OK.

Renaming Files and Directories

Renaming a file or directory with an FTP program is also fairly easy. Still, depending on the type of computer you use, you may need to use slightly different steps.

In just about any Windows program, right-click on the file or directory name, and then select the Rename or similar option from the shortcut menu. Type in your new name, and then press Enter or click on a different item.

On the Mac, you can usually rename files and directories just as you normally would. Click on the file or directory name, wait for the name to become editable, and then type in a new name. Press Enter.

Creating Directories on the Server

Creating new directories is fairly straightforward. Choose the Create Directory, New Directory, or similar option on your program's toolbar or menu. Enter the name for the directory if prompted. Otherwise, change the default name given to the directory. That's it.

Chapter 9. Working with the Web's Search Engines and Directories

All this talk of the wonderful resources on the Internet may have you wondering how you can find things for yourself. After all, there are few signposts and no road maps to cyberspace. So how do you find anything?

I suppose that one way to find stuff on the Internet would be to wander aimlessly from webpage to webpage following links that looked interesting and hoping to eventually find what you are looking for. Unfortunately, with millions of resources out there, you could wander the Web a very long time and still not find the information you need to write that research paper, finish your business proposal, or teach your child about the world.

Another way to find stuff on the Internet would be to enlist the help of search engines and Web directories. A *search engine* is a tool that you can use to search for Internet resources by keyword. A *Web directory* is a tool that you can use to browse for Internet resources by subject area.

Finding Stuff on the Web

In the early days of the Web, search engines were simple tools for finding information by using indexes. Much like the index of your favorite computer book, the purpose of the index was to make finding information possible by using keywords. Rather than the page references used in traditional indexes, Web indexes had hypertext links that you could click on to access the information at websites around the world.

Over the years, search engines evolved. Today, the best search engines are complex applications that use advanced techniques to put millions of webpages at the fingertips of Web users. Often, these advanced search engines have descriptive names that hint at the techniques the search engine uses to index webpages, such as *spider* or *crawler*.

Working with Search Engines

No matter what label you use to identify a search engine, the fundamental purpose of a search engine is generally to index websites in a way that allows people to use keywords to find webpages that interest them. To do this, search engines rely on an indexer to ferret out the pages at a website and then create indexed references to those pages. After the pages are indexed, anyone can use the front-end search process to find the pages.

> **Note:** All this talk about webpages may have you wondering if you can use search engines to find other types of information. The answer is yes. Search engines are also used to create indexes to other types of Internet resources and information, such as pictures and videos.

When you search on the Web, you will use form fields to enter information, make selections, and start the search. If you jaunt over to Bing at http://www.bing.com, you'll find an input field, several radio buttons, and a Search button (see Figure 9-1). The input field is used to enter what you want to search for. The radio buttons are used to toggle between various options. When you click on the Search button, the search engine uses the parameters you've entered to find matching references.

Figure 9-1

Using a search engine

When you search using the keywords "funny cat videos" you get a list of results like those shown in Figure 9-2. As you can see, the results of a search are usually displayed according to their relevancy to the search parameters that you entered. The higher the relevancy, the greater the probability that the search results contain what you are looking for.

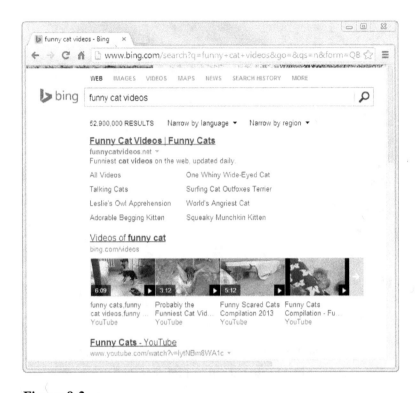

Figure 9-2

The results of a search

Most search engines display references to the top 10 or 20 pages that match your search parameters. Successive groups of matching pages are also available, but you have to follow a link to another results page. At Bing, you can click on the Next link found at the top and bottom of the results page to see additional pages that might be a match for your search.

Often, the matching pages are described using the page title and a brief description taken from the page itself. Most commercial search engines allow you to customize the search and how search results are displayed. In advanced searches, you can also specify how strictly you want the search engine to match your parameters to webpages, the number of possible matches to display in each results page and more.

Comparing Search Engines and Directory Lists

Search engines and directory lists are very different. When you look for information with a search engine, you use keywords. When you look for information at a directory listing, you search by following links to pages within the directory site. Your search starts by clicking on a broad category, such as entertainment, and you eventually drill down to a very specific subject, such as movie reviews.

One of the best-known directory lists is Yahoo! (http://www.yahoo.com). When you visit the Yahoo! home page, the left side of the window has a listing of the top-level categories of information available at the site. If you select the Sports category, you end up on the http://sports.yahoo.com/ page.

Yahoo! also makes use of a search engine. Using search, you can find information faster, without having to spend time following links from a broad category to specific articles. Once you've found something that looks interesting, all you have to do is click on the link provided to visit any of the millions of websites listed at Yahoo!.

Other search engines and web directories you might want to try include:

- **AOL**   http://www.aol.com

- **Excite** http://www.excite.com
- **Google** http://www.google.com
- **Lycos** http://www.lycos.com

Searching the Web: Step by Step

You'll quickly discover that search engines and Web directories are very easy to use. There's not much to entering a keyword and pressing a button or clicking on category links to find information. Yet with millions of Internet resources, your search may turn up more information than you can use—or it may turn up lots of extraneous information that doesn't relate to what you are looking for. Instead of wading through hundreds of pages of search results, you will often want to refine your search techniques.

Search Basics

Most of the top search engines index hundreds of millions of webpages. Anytime you have hundreds of millions of anything, there are bound to be a lot of similar listings. That search using the keywords "Funny cat videos" at Bing returned over 52,900,000 results. Instead of wading through all those listings, it would be much simpler to refine the search using additional keywords, which is the advice most search engines give you on their help pages. The idea is that if you use precise keywords, you should be able to narrow your search and get stronger matches.

For example, if you are looking for sports equipment, you could narrow the results by looking for sports equipment companies, sports equipment stores, or some other related topic. Let's say you were looking for sports equipment stores—you could use the keywords "sports equipment stores." On the main Bing page, enter the keywords in the input field provided. By default, the Bing search engine looks at its Web index, so you don't need to change the default settings. Click on the Search button to start the search. Huh? The search results say 52 million pages match those parameters. What happened?

Unfortunately, Bing and most other search engines look for matches using all the keywords provided. Because of this, pages containing any or all of your keywords are considered to be a match. To truly narrow the search using precise keywords, you need to use search operators. You'll learn more about search operators later. For now, let's go back and try that initial search again.

Let's see, what were the previous search parameters? Oh yes, I remember, sports equipment stores. So start a new search, only this time enter the keywords "sports equipment stores in Washington state." Huh? The search results show 70 million matches and last time there were 52 million matches. What's going on?

Well, as before the search engine used all of the keywords you entered. Because of this, a search for "sports equipment stores in Washington" yields even more results than "sports equipment stores."

Using Search Operators

Search operators allow you to refine and narrow your search. Using search operators, you could tell a search engine that you only want to see pages that contain all your keywords. You could also tell a search engine to match resources containing specific keywords but not others.

Generally, you use a plus sign (+) to indicate words that must appear and a minus sign (-) to indicate words that must not appear. Do not put a space between the operator and the keyword. Here are some examples:

- +sports +equipment +stores   Search results must contain all three keywords.
- +sports +equipment -companies   Search results must contain the keywords sports and equipment. Reject any of these pages that contain the keyword companies.

Another handy search operator is the double quotation mark. You can use this operator to identify words that must appear together, such as "football helmet" or "sports memorabilia."

The difference between a search for *+sports +memorabilia* and a search for *"sports memorabilia"* is subtle but important. In the first case, you are searching for two keywords that must be in the document but don't have to appear together. In the second case, you are searching for two keywords that must appear together as a phrase.

In a perfect world all search engines would support these three easy-to-use operators. Unfortunately, you will find that searching the Web isn't an exact science. Before someone dreamed up these wonderful operators, most search engines relied on operators called AND and OR. These are called *Boolean operators* and must be typed in all caps with a space separating them from other keywords.

The AND operator is used to join words that must appear in the matching documents. The OR operator is used to specify an alternative keyword and is often the default behavior. Here are some examples:

- sports AND equipment AND stores   Search results must contain all three keywords.
- sports OR equipment   Search results must contain at least one of the keywords. Because this is often default behavior, you do not have to specify the OR operator.

Oh yeah, and how does our original search work now? Well, give it a try. If you enter *+sports +equipment +stores +washington*, Bing returns 3.8 million results. Not great, but substantially less than the original search and substantially more targeted.

For even better results, enter *"sports equipment store"* or *"sports equipment store" "Seattle, Washington"*. These searches return 130,000 and 40,500 results respectively and you'll be more likely to find exactly what you are looking for.

Problems You May Have While Searching

Anytime you don't obtain the results you expect, you should ask yourself what went wrong. Search engines aren't perfect. They can only search on what you give them. They can't find resources that they haven't indexed. Worse, they will rarely tell you when a search operator you've used is not valid.

When you don't get the results you expect:

- **Check your keywords for typos**   If you meant to use the keyword "music" but you typed in "msuic" instead, the search engine won't know that you made an error. As a result, your search probably won't return any results. What you'll find instead is a mostly empty page that should contain your original search parameters.
- **Look at your keywords**   Search parameters are great, but it is easy to get too many results or too few results. Don't use vague keywords. To focus your search, try using two or three descriptive keywords.
- **Ensure the operators are valid**   A search engine that doesn't support the operators may search for instances of words that occur exactly as you type them. As a result, you get distorted results.
- **Try a different search engine**   Although search engines index lots of resources, no search engine indexes every Internet resource available. You may want to try your search elsewhere.

Note: Most search sites will have a help page that explains how to perform a search at the site. Usually, you will find a link to this help page next to the search query box.

Chapter 10. Finding Your Way Around the Web

Until now, I've focused primarily on Internet tools. You've explored browsers, email programs, and much more. By learning how to use these tools, you learned how to access everything the Net has to offer. Before you finish up, there is one area that you must explore to fully understand what the Internet has to offer: the Web.

Finding anything in the maze of the Web would be impossible without a little help. Thus, my goal in this chapter is to help you discover the resources you'll use time and again. These resources will help you find businesses around the world and in your own backyard; get in touch with long-lost friends; learn about places you've never been; and discover what is fun, free, and cool.

Search engines and Web directories are terrific tools for finding information and resources. You can rely on a search engine such as Bing to return a list of sites that match your search parameters. You can rely on a Web directory such as Yahoo! to help you find websites by subject. As wonderful as search engines and directories are, however, you may discover that it is sometimes hard to find exactly what you are looking for. Sometimes, you may not want to browse hundreds of different websites. Wouldn't it be great if you could go straight to the top website on a particular subject? Well, you can, and you will use Web guides to help you.

Finding the best the Web has to offer is one thing; finding the best the real world has to offer is another thing. Because you may also want to find the best places to visit in your own backyard, you'll also find information on regional guides. A regional guide can help you plan your weekend, give you information on a city you plan to visit, and even tell you which restaurant at which you may want to dine.

No Road Maps—But Lots of Guides

Web guides provide pointers to the best the Web has to offer. Think of a guide as something you might buy to help you learn about a country you are visiting. After all, you wouldn't take a dream vacation without a little planning, so why visit the Web and wander aimlessly when you can use a guide to help you find the interesting places to visit?

Most Web guides center on site reviews. Some reviews are fairly extensive and closely resemble feature articles you may find in a magazine. Other reviews are brief and to the point.

To help you discern the best websites from the good or the good–but-could-be-better, some Web guides rate featured sites in several categories. One guide may rate sites in presentation, content, and the overall experience of visiting the site. Another guide may rate sites in content, design, and personality. Either way, the scores in each category are usually combined and become the site's overall rating. Contrary to what you might think, the websites with the fancy graphics and multimedia don't always have the best ratings. In fact, some of the most highly rated websites have mostly text.

As with directories, most guides can be searched in two ways:

- By category
- By keyword

When you search by category, you follow links from a broad category to a progressively more focused category. Here, the category headings are designed to help you find sites that might interest you. A keyword search in a guide is handled in a very different manner. Rather than follow links, you use a search interface to find categories and listings within the guide. If the keywords that you enter lead to several different categories, you see category headers. If the keywords that you enter lead to a specific listing, you see either the listing itself or the page of which the listing is a part. Here, your search parameters play the most important role in helping you find sites that might interest you.

So You'd Like a Guided Tour: Start Here

Looking for a guided tour to the Web? You will definitely want to start with the best Web guides. As you will quickly learn, most Web guides combine their website reviews with news, information, and other services. Two guides to get you started are C|Net and Web 100.

C | Net: The Computer Network

News, information, and resources

http://www.cnet.com/

C|Net is like an information headquarters. You will find feature-length articles on computer-related topics, headline news from the computer industry, and website reviews. C|Net hosts many other websites and services, such as Download.Com. Although these sites are found at other Web addresses, they are all a part of C|Net's computer network and as such, all of them are accessible from C|Net's main website.

Web 100

Guide to top 100 Web Sites

http://www.web100.com/

The Web 100 is a guide to the top 100 of the Web. You can browse the top 100 photos, the top 100 viral videos, the top 100 websites and more.

Guides Are Great—But What about Local Stuff?

The Web is the great equalizer when it comes to putting information and resources at your fingertips. You know you can rely on the Web to conduct research, find product information, read about killer whales, and lots of other things that seem a world away. Yet when it comes to finding information in your own hometown or neighborhood, the Web isn't always the place you would look—but it certainly should be, especially if you live near a major metropolitan area.

Guides to local information are called regional guides. Because regional guides usually focus on a specific city or metropolitan area, these guides are also referred to as city or metro guides. Most regional guides provide extensive community information, so extensive in fact that you could use a regional guide to plan your weekend, a trip to Seattle, or the big move this fall.

Some regional guides are guides in the true sense of the word. These more traditional guides feature the kind of extensive information you would expect from a Frommier's travel guide. You will find information on restaurants, outdoor recreation, entertainment, shopping, and maps. You could use this information to find a five-star pizzeria or a classy jazz club.

Many regional guides also feature current events, news, and weather. Up-to-the-minute information is great when you want to see what is playing at the movies, get a baseball schedule, or check the weekend forecast.

Regional guides don't always develop their own content. Instead of an actual article or review, you may find links that lead to other sites where the information is published. Although it may seem as if guides that primarily provide links are at a disadvantage, this is not always the case. Often guides with less detail cover many different regions rather than a single region. In a way, these guides sacrifice detail for more areas of coverage.

Technically, a site that doesn't create its own material is more of a directory than a guide. The difference between a true guide and a directory is more apparent when you look at the level of detailed information available. Regional guides usually have detailed information on a specific city or metropolitan area. Regional directories usually cover many different regions, but have less detailed information.

The way you search or browse regional guides depends on what you are looking for. Because most services that create regional guides support more than one area, the best way to find a specific guide is to start on the service's main site. You'll find a service called Mapquest Local at *http://local.mapquest.com*. Yahoo! also has a local service called Yahoo! Local and it's at *http://local.yahoo.com*.

Once you are at the website for the regional guide, you will usually be able to search for things that interest you (just as you would in a search engine) or browse the site by category. If you were in the mood for pizza, you could browse the restaurants section. If you wanted to check local theaters and show times, you could browse the movies section.

Chapter 11. Finding People and Businesses

Just about everyone has used a White Pages or Yellow Pages directory at one time or another. Every year phone companies around the world kill a few million trees in their efforts to deliver these enormous tomes to our doorsteps and every year we throw out the old directories and bring in the new. Despite the thousands of listings crammed into a typical directory, the directory is really only good for your local area. If you want to find the phone number of a business in the next state, you have to call Information and pay a fee for the service.

Web-based White Pages and Yellow Pages directories change all that by providing extensive listings for cities throughout the United States and the world. You can use a White Pages directory to find the phone number of a distant relative as easily as you can find the phone number of a neighbor down the street. Using a Yellow Pages directory, you can find a business in Miami as easily as you can find a business in Boston.

Finding Your Long-Lost Friends in the White Pages

Millions of people are connected to the online world. They have phone numbers, email addresses, and home pages. Finding out who's wired in and who's not is what White Pages directories are all about. Unlike the White Pages of your phone book, which have listings for your local area only, Web-based White Pages directories cover entire countries, allowing you to search the world without having to know the area code or country code of the person you are trying to reach.

Getting to Know the White Pages

Although the White Pages do contain business listings, White Pages directories are primarily about people. Just as traditional White Pages directories are moving beyond phone numbers and addresses, so are Web-based White Pages directories. You might find not only someone's phone number in these directories but also their email address and home page URL.

Because White Pages directories make finding people anywhere in the world so easy, their popularity is rivaled only by that of the major search engines and the best Web guides. That said, White Pages directories have their drawbacks, just like any other type of directory or search site. With millions of listings in a typical directory, you will usually find multiple listings for the same name, which means you generally have to rely on geographic information to find the person you are looking for. Further, because our world isn't static, information about people changes every day, which means you can sometimes encounter outdated listings. However, it is much easier to update a Web-based directory than a printed directory, which means that the online directory will often be more accurate than its printed cousin.

Speaking of cousins, if you ever want to find a long-lost cousin, relative, or friend, a White Pages directory should be your first choice to aid your quest. Some directories have millions of listings, putting an enormous database at your fingertips. I've used White Pages directories to find friends I hadn't spoken with in years. All you need to get started is a person's name and some inkling of where the person may live.

Searching Using White Pages

To find a phone number and street address, you need to enter any information you know on the person, such as their first name, last name and the state where you think they reside. If the person has a common name, you may want to narrow the search by being more specific. However, narrowing the search too much won't help you find the person you are looking for. People often move from city to city and from state to state.

When it comes to White Pages directories, a few stand out from the crowd, including:

- **DexKnows WhitePages**
  http://dexknows.whitepages.com/
- **AnyWho**   http://www.anywho.com/
- **WhitePages**   http://www.whitepages.com/

Whether you use one over another will depend largely on the area the directory serves and your personal preference.

Finding Businesses in the Yellow Pages

Millions of businesses offer products and services on the Web. The sites that help Web users make sense of all these offerings are the Yellow Pages directories. Because these search and directory sites are tailored for businesses, you can usually search for specific businesses by company name, location, and industry as well as the products and services that the companies offer.

Getting to Know the Yellow Pages

Yellow Pages directories are the essential guides to business on and off the Net. As with White Pages directories, Yellow Pages directories have moved beyond the traditional information found in your favorite phone book. Because of this, in addition to telephone numbers and street addresses, you will usually find email addresses and home page URLs.

It should come as no surprise that many Yellow Pages directories offer additional services to businesses. These premium services allow businesses to customize their listings and provide additional information. The combination of premium listings and standard listings often explains why you may be able to find lots of information on one company and not much on another company.

The good news is that because of the corporate dollars involved, Yellow Pages are some of the best-maintained and best-organized directories available. Visit a site like the QwestDex (http://www.qwestdex.com) and you'll see what I mean immediately.

When you combine product information with business listings, you get a Yellow Pages directory that can help you with lots of different tasks. However, some Yellow Pages directories have a more traditional style. Instead of all these extras, you may only be able to find business listings.

Searching the Yellow Pages

Searching for a company's name or products is a fairly straight forward process. You access the appropriate area of the Yellow Pages directory, and then enter your search parameters. For example, you could enter Bob's Burgers as the business name and Seattle, Washington as the location to search.

Although a searching for a business by name is fairly easy, searching for a business listing can be tricky. The reason is that you may not know the name of the company you are looking for. Instead, you may only know the type of business or service you need. Here, you would have to search by category or subject area. Although each directory has its own unique categories, most categories are similar to the various subject headings of your phone book. For example, if you wanted to search for builders in your area, you would enter "builders" and then provide the area to search near, such as Orlando, Florida.

When it comes to Yellow Pages directories, a few stand out from the crowd, including:

- **DexKnows**   http://www.dexknows.com/
- **WhoWhere**   http://www.whowhere.com/
- **Yellow**   http://www.yellow.com/
- **YellowPages**   http://www.yellowpages.com/

As with White Pages directories, whether you use one over another will depend largely on the area the directory serves and your personal preference.

Chapter 12. Going Shopping Online

Shopping online is fun—name an activity you can do in your bathrobe and slippers that isn't fun. Just think about it, you don't have to drive to the mall, fight for a parking space, or deal with crowds. You can shop hundreds of stores for bargains without ever having to leave the comfort of your favorite chair. When you want to compare prices, you don't have to walk from one side of the mall to the other, either. All you have to do is point, click, and maybe punch a few keys on your keyboard.

What You Need to Know Before You Shop

The Internet is a bargain hunter's bonanza. But before you head off to the virtual shopping mall, there are a few things you should know.

Virtual Shopping Carts

Online shopping is much like shopping at your favorite mall. You can window shop, look for sales, and do all the things you would normally do at a real store. When you find something you like, you can add the item to your shopping cart—well, a virtual shopping cart.

A virtual shopping cart is similar to a real shopping cart. You can add items to the shopping cart and take inventory of what's there. If you later decide you don't want an item, you can take it out of your shopping cart. Then when you are ready to make a purchase, you can proceed to the checkout counter.

Adding items to your shopping cart is easy. You browse the store shelves until you find something you like, such as the book shown in Figure 12-1, and then you click on a button or follow a link to add the item to your shopping cart. In the example, you would click on the Add To Bag button.

Figure 12-1

Sometimes you can place an item in your shopping cart by using an Add button.

Next, you may have to specify the quantity of the item to purchase. The default quantity is usually one, but you can use the input fields or buttons provided to change the default value. If you wanted to purchase two books, you would change the input field shown in Figure 12-2 to 2.

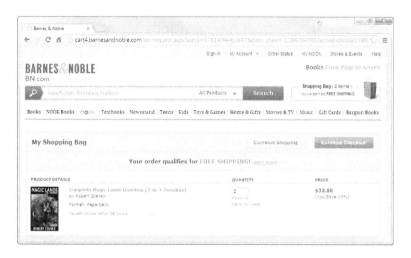

Figure 12-2

After you add an item to your shopping cart, you may have to specify the purchase quantity.

Because you may want to buy more than one item, you can continue shopping. Go back to the store's search page or home page to find more stuff. When you are ready, you can take a final inventory of items in your shopping cart. Usually, the store will provide a button such as the Shopping Bar button found in the upper right corner of Figure 12-2.

Anytime you are viewing the contents of the shopping cart, you should be able to remove items as well. Most of the time, you can delete an item by changing the purchase quantity to zero. You may also be able to click on a button or link to remove items. When you are ready to make your purchase, proceed to the checkout counter.

At BN.Com, you can proceed to the checkout counter in one of two ways. When you are adding items to your shopping cart, there is a Continue Checkout button. Elsewhere in the store, there is a Shopping Bag button that you can click on to view the contents of your shopping cart and continue to checkout if wanted.

Store Accounts and Security

The checkout counter is where things get a bit different. After all, you are shopping in a virtual store. The clerk can't see you. You can't pass the clerk a $20 bill. The clerk needs a way to identify you as the purchaser and a way to know the bill will be paid, which is where store accounts come into the picture.

Most online stores ask you to create a customer account the first time you want to check out and make a purchase. By this time, your shopping cart usually contains the items you intend to purchase. The basic information you'll need for the account is your personal contact information, which normally includes:

- Full name
- Street Address
- Phone Number
- Email Address
- Preferred payment method

If the item is a gift, you may also have to specify a shipping address. As an incentive to purchase online, many stores offer gift wrapping, especially around the holidays.

Anytime you select a preferred payment method, you may also have to specify a credit card number. Although a little alarm bell may be ringing in your head right now, keep in mind you don't have to use a credit card. You don't even have to have a credit card issued by a bank. Most online stores allow you to pay by gift card, by pre-paid credit card or by using an alternative payment option, such as PayPal.com.

Just about everyone is wary the first time someone asks for a credit card number online—and well they should be. Security is a big issue in online shopping. Every purchase you make with a credit card should be handled by a secure Web server. The secure server should encrypt all transactions. While encryption will hide your credit card information from snoopers, however, it will not protect you from unscrupulous merchants. For this reason, you should only make purchases from established online shops run by credible merchants.

A credible merchant isn't necessarily the one with the fancy graphics or the high power design at his online shop. The size of the website or the number of items for sale doesn't really make a difference either. Thousands of credible Ma and Pa shops are on the Web. Some of these shops are really small and specialize in selling a few unique items that you can't get elsewhere.

Instead of focusing on glitz, glamour and size, focus on the shop itself. Look closely at the information pages at the website, such as the company background page, the customer information pages and the help documentation. These pages should tell you a great deal about the merchant. Here is what you should look for:

- **Merchant location**   Dealing with international shipping of goods can be a hassle. You generally want to shop stores in your own country. While you're looking at the merchant's contact information, write down the address and telephone number so you have this information for future reference.

- **Payment options**   Most credible merchants will accept a variety of payment options which may include credit cards, gift cards or some type of electronic cash. E-cash merchants such as PayPal.com are popular alternatives for electronic transactions on the Web.

- **Payment security**   If the merchant accepts credit card or e-cash payments, payments should be made using a secure Web server. As stated previously in the book, most browsers uses a locked padlock symbol to tell you that you are on a secure server. Regardless of what the merchant tells you, never send your credit card or e-cash account information in an email message. Email isn't secure unless you encrypt it.

- **Affiliations/awards**   Affiliations with trade organizations, associations or guilds can be a good indicator that a merchant is legitimate. Merchants that have been around for a while should have a track record in the form of awards or press releases.

When you finish filling out the purchase form, the online store will use the information to create an account for you. To allow you to purchase items in the future without having to go through the account creation process again, the online store may ask you to select an account name and password. This account name and password should be unique for each store you shop at. For future use, keep a record of all your online accounts and be sure to write down your account name and password.

Shipping and Currency Gotchas

The most common gotchas for online shopping come at checkout time, when you find that an online store you thought was in your home country isn't. Just because a virtual store has writing in your native tongue or is published under recognizable name doesn't mean the store is located in your home country. The Internet is a global network with computers in many different countries. Anytime you shop in a foreign country, there may be additional charges. These additional charges may include extra shipping fees, taxes, and perhaps even tariffs.

Because of these extra fees, that bargain you found may not be such a bargain. The good news is that most online stores list all the fees up front—if they don't, shop elsewhere. A good online store will tell you the total purchase price including shipping, handling, and any applicable taxes or other fees.

Another gotcha that comes into play when you shop in foreign countries is the currency exchange rate. An online shop may not have a price converter that tells you how much an item is going to cost in your currency. If you live in the United States and want to purchase something from an online store in Canada, you'll have to covert U.S. dollars to Canadian dollars.

Just because you see a price in dollars, that doesn't mean the price is in U.S. dollars. Many countries use the dollar sign symbol. So unless the merchant specifically says U.S. dollars, you won't know for sure if you are dealing in U.S. dollars, Canadian dollars, or Australian dollars—or maybe Hong Kong dollars or something even stranger.

Basically, you will want to convert the prices to your currency so you will know how much you have to pay. If you use a credit card to make a purchase, you don't have to worry about making a payment in a specific currency. The charge will appear on the credit card bill in your own currency.

Buying Books Online

Nothing is better than browsing the aisles of a bookstore on a lazy Sunday afternoon. If you are like me, you can spend hours just browsing and every once in a while, you'll take a book off the shelf and thumb through it. Thumbing through a book is half the fun. So when you think about buying books online, you may wonder if it'll still be as much fun. The answer is a definitive yes.

When you shop for books online, you can browse the virtual aisles of an online shop book by book. Many online bookstores have feature sections covering the latest and best books in a particular genre, where you will often find commentary, reviews, and a whole lot more. Because these stores want customers to come back time and again, many online bookstores are updated daily, making them the place to catch up on the latest book gossip.

Anyone in a hurry can search for books instead of browsing around. Generally, you will be able to search by subject area, author name, book title, and ISBN. From the search results, you should be able to access a book information page. Sometimes this page will include customer comments and ratings, which allows you to get the inside track on what readers think about the book.

If expert comments and customer buzz aren't enough to hook you, wait till you see the discounts most online bookstores offer. The top online bookstores include:

- **Barnes and Noble**   US-based, http://www.barnesandnoble.com/
- **Books-A-Million**   US-based, http://www.booksamillion.com/
- **Indigo**   Canada-based, http://chapters.indigo.ca/
- **Mighty Ape**   Australia-based, http://www.mightyape.com.au
- **Waterstones**   UK-based, http://www.waterstones.com/

Music Shopping Online

If you're not interested in shopping for books online, you may want to tune in to music shopping online. As much as you may love to buy music, you've probably haven't been in the music section of a department store in a long time.

Good news. On the Net, you don't have to worry about a store not having a title you are looking for or about overpaying. Most online music stores stock thousands of titles and allow you to order any available title. If you don't like the price in one music store, you can check the price in another store with a few mouse clicks.

As with online bookstores, online music stores want to give you an experience you can't get elsewhere. You'll find that the best online music stores publish music news, reviews, and industry gossip. Stores even let you listen to clips of music from songs before you buy them. The first time you try this, you may have to follow the store's instructions for updating your browser to play music.

You can shop for music in much the same way you shop for books. You can browse the store's aisles by category, or check for sales or weekly specials. If you are in a hurry, you can also perform a search. Usually online music stores allow you to search by artist name, album title, song title, or record label.

Some of online music stores you may want to check out include:

- **Artist Direct**   http://www.artistdirect.com/
- **E-music**   http://www.emusic.com/
- **iTunes**   https://www.apple.com/itunes/
- **Spotify**   http://www.spotify.com/

Finding Shopping Malls Online

Although books and music are two major categories of items you may want to shop for online, the online shopping experience doesn't stop there. You'll find everything from groceries to flowers to cars being sold online. In fact, if you can buy it in a physical store, you can buy it in a virtual store.

The best place to buy groceries, flowers, cars and more is in a virtual mall. A virtual mall, like a real mall, is a collection of stores. Some virtual malls are huge, with thousands of stores selling many different types of goods. However, don't let size fool you. On the Web, size isn't as important as usability.

The best online malls are easy to use, fun, and friendly. You should be able to browse the stores in the mall easily. The stores should have interesting aisles. You should be able to add items to a community shopping cart that can be used throughout the mall, and then check out when you are ready.

Although I've painted a picture of the ideal online mall, you will find that not all stores in a mall use a community shopping cart. The reason for this is that some stores sell services or information that doesn't easily fit into the umbrella of other stores. A few other stores may prefer to sell their products on their own website or through existing channels, such as the telephone or mail order. Find your next favorite online shopping mall using the search engines and web directories I discussed earlier.

About the Author

William R. Stanek (http://www.williamstanek.com/) has more than 20 years of hands-on experience with advanced programming and development. He is a leading technology expert, an award-winning author, and a pretty-darn-good instructional trainer. Over the years, his practical advice has helped millions of programmers, developers, and network engineers all over the world. His current and books include Windows 8 Administration Pocket Consultant, Windows Server 2012 Pocket Consultant and SQL Server 2012 Pocket Consultant.

William has been involved in the commercial Internet community since 1991. His core business and technology experience comes from more than 11 years of military service. He has substantial experience in developing server technology, encryption, and Internet solutions. He has written many technical white papers and training courses on a wide variety of topics. He frequently serves as a subject matter expert and consultant.

William has an MS with distinction in information systems and a BS in computer science, magna cum laude. He is proud to have served in the Persian Gulf War as a combat crewmember on an electronic warfare aircraft. He flew on numerous combat missions into Iraq and was awarded nine medals for his wartime service, including one of the United States of America's highest flying honors, the Air Force Distinguished Flying Cross. Currently, he resides in the Pacific Northwest with his wife and children.

William recently rediscovered his love of the great outdoors. When he's not writing, he can be found hiking, biking, backpacking, traveling, or trekking in search of adventure with his family!

Find William on Twitter at www.twitter.com/WilliamStanek and on Facebook at www.facebook.com/William.Stanek.Author.

www.ingramcontent.com/pod-product-compliance
Lightning Source LLC
La Vergne TN
LVHW051327050326
832903LV00031B/3403